Divine Feminine Unveiled

HONORING SACRED FEMININITY, EMPOWERING WOMEN'S WISDOM, AND EMBODYING GRACE FOR THE MODERN WOMAN

HEATHER DOLSON

HEATHER ON HEALTH

Copyright © 2024 by Heather Dolson and Heather on Health

All rights reserved.

No portion of this book may be reproduced in any form without written permission from the publisher or author, except as permitted by U.S. copyright law.

Although I am a nurse, I am not your nurse. The medical and health information provided in this book is for general, informational, and educational purposes only and is not a substitute for professional advice. Accordingly, before taking any actions based upon such information, I encourage you to consult with the appropriate professionals. I do not provide any kind of medical/health advice.

Contents

Introduction	1
1. Decoding Divine Feminine	4
2. Embracing Your Feminine Energy	14
3. Archetypes of the Divine Feminine	28
4. The Divine Balance: Feminine and Masculine Energies	43
5. The Sacred Art of Self-Care	53
6. The Divine Feminine: Shaping Relationships with Authenticity and Empathy	64
7. Divine Feminine: Healing Emotional Wounds and Cultivating Resilience	76
8. The Divine Feminine: Dancing with Grace, Flowing with Life	88
9. Manifesting with the Divine Feminine: Turning Dreams into Reality	110
10. The Divine Feminine Sisterhood: United in Strength, Resilience and Love	121
11. Divine Feminine: Embracing the Sacred in Everyday Life	131

12. Divine Feminine: Becoming the Pathmaker	141
Conclusion	150
Your Reviews Matter	153
A Gift for my Readers	155
References	156
About the Author	160
Also by Heather Dolson	162

Introduction

Have you ever sensed a soft, yet profound whisper that seemed to echo from the depths of your very being? A whisper that, when attended to, unfolds itself into truth, wisdom, power, and love? This, dear one, is the whisper of the Divine Feminine.

In a world that often feels fast-paced and out of balance, this whisper can seem faint, almost imperceptible, drowned out by the clamor of daily duties, responsibilities, and external expectations. But trust me when I tell you, it is always there. Patiently waiting. Gently nudging. Inviting you to remember, embrace and reclaim the sacredness that resides deep within you.

This book is designed to help amplify that whisper. My vision is to guide you on a transformative journey of self-discovery and self-love. A journey that will help you reconnect with the innate wisdom and power of being a woman, and give you the tools to embody the Divine Feminine in every aspect of your life.

I have devoted years to exploring the intricate beauty of the feminine, weaving together threads from Kundalini and Tantra yoga, exploring my sensuality, and practicing and facilitating Sensual Embodiment (TM). While my journey is uniquely mine, the wisdom and insights I've gained have the potential to illuminate your path, too.

I'm Heather, your fellow traveler on this path, and I want to share a bit of my journey with you. As a single mother, I've faced the challenges of juggling parenthood, career, and personal growth. There were moments when I felt overwhelmed, stressed out, and burdened by the weight of responsibilities, and this need to be hyper-independent and prove something. In my quest to do it all, I found myself disconnected from the very essence of my femininity.

My journey involved exploring the feminine's intricate beauty and healing my relationship with the masculine. As a hyper-independent person, I had to learn to embrace receptivity and flow, qualities often associated with the feminine. One of the most difficult things for me was to ask for help. I had this belief I had to do it all and I would be a burden if I admitted I needed help. Part of my journey has been realizing we all need people and while our lives are uniquely our own, we are meant to thrive in community. It was a transformative process, a dance between the assertiveness of the masculine and the nurturing embrace of the feminine.

Now, the sacred journey awaits you. It will not always be easy. There will be moments of struggle, of self-doubt, of resistance. But remember, like a lotus flower that grows through the mud to reach the surface, it is through these very challenges that we grow and awaken to our true selves.

As you turn each page, may you find comfort in knowing that you are not alone. We are in this together, embarking on a journey to uncover and celebrate the Divine Feminine, the Goddess within us all. I am excited to share this journey with you, to learn and grow together, and to witness the magnificent transformation that awaits.

Welcome, dear one, to this sacred journey. Let the Divine Feminine whisper grow into the beautiful symphony of your life.

Chapter One

Decoding Divine Feminine

A quiet sunrise, the gentle ebb and flow of ocean waves, the nurturing embrace of a lover - what do these all have in common? They are all expressions of the Divine Feminine, a universal energy that permeates our world and ourselves. But what exactly is the Divine Feminine? To truly understand its essence, we must take a step back and explore its historical context, its interpretation across different cultures, and its relationship with spirituality.

The True Meaning of Divine Feminine

The Divine Feminine is not a new concept. In fact, it is as ancient as life itself. Its roots stretch back to prehistoric times when our ancestors worshipped the Great Mother, a deity who embodied the earth, fertility, and the life-giving properties of nature. They recognized the Divine Feminine in the cycles of the moon, the seasons, and even in their own bodies.

Over time, as societies evolved and patriarchal systems began to dominate, reverence for the Divine Feminine declined. However, the Divine Feminine never disappeared completely. It continued to exist, subtly woven into the fabric of our collective consciousness, waiting to be rediscovered and reclaimed.

In today's world, we are witnessing a resurgence in the appreciation for the Divine Feminine. More and more women - and men - are feeling called to connect with this powerful energy and integrate it into their lives.

Historical Context of Divine Feminine

The Divine Feminine has been known by many names throughout history. In ancient Greece, she was revered as Gaia, the mother of all life. In Hindu tradition, she is the Shakti, the vital cosmic energy that animates all beings.

In Early Christian Gnostic texts, she is Sophia, the embodiment of wisdom. In indigenous cultures around the world, she is the Earth Mother, the source of all nourishment and life. Despite the cultural variations, a common thread runs through all these traditions: the Divine Feminine is a source of life, wisdom, and transformative power.

Divine Feminine in Different Cultures

The Divine Feminine is not confined to any one culture or religion. It is a universal energy that transcends geographical boundaries and cultural differences.

In Buddhism, the Divine Feminine is embodied in the figure of Kuan Yin, the Goddess of Compassion. She is often depicted pouring a stream of healing water, the "Water of Life," from a small vase, symbolizing the purifying power of compassion.

In the Yoruba tradition of West Africa, the Divine Feminine is represented by various Orishas, or deities, such as Yemoja, the goddess of the ocean and motherhood, and Oya, the goddess of winds, tempests, and transformation.

In Native American cultures, the Divine Feminine is often associated with the Earth and nature. For instance, the Hopi people speak of Spider Woman, the deity who, according to their creation story, wove the universe into existence.

These examples illustrate the vast and diverse ways in which the Divine Feminine has been recognized and honored across cultures.

Divine Feminine and Spirituality

The Divine Feminine is closely linked to spirituality. After all, it is a divine energy, a sacred aspect of the universal life force that pervades all existence. Connecting with the Divine Feminine is, in essence, a spiritual practice. It involves awakening to our inherent divinity and recognizing the sacredness in ourselves and in the world around us.

In spiritual circles, the Divine Feminine is often associated with qualities such as intuition, compassion, creativity, and emotional intelligence. It represents the aspect of the self that is nurturing, intuitive, and receptive. It is the inner wisdom that guides us, the nurturing love that heals us, and the creative force that inspires us.

The Divine Feminine invites us to honor our emotions, to listen to our intuition, and to nurture our inner self. It encourages us to form deep connections - with ourselves, with others, and with the natural world. It calls us to live authentically, to speak our truth, and to honor our unique path.

The exploration of the Divine Feminine is not about rejecting or diminishing the masculine. On the contrary, it is about achieving balance. Just as day balances night and winter balances summer, so too does the Divine Feminine balance the Divine Masculine. Both are necessary, both are valuable, and both are worthy of honor and respect.

This depiction brings to mind a poignant exchange I shared with a spiritual guide. It centered around my son and the challenges he faced, particularly stemming from his father's absence in his life. As a mother grappling with my own emotions, I found myself at a loss for adequate answers to his probing questions. Sensing my struggle, my mentor offered invaluable counsel, urging me to seek professional assistance for my son, a decision I ultimately made. But it was her profound insight that resonated deeply: "Until you heal your relationship with the masculine, you'll carry the burden of feeling inadequate." I will touch upon this further in the book.

Understanding the Divine Feminine is a key step in our journey towards wholeness and balance. As we awaken to the Divine Feminine within us, we begin to see the world with new eyes. We start to perceive the sacredness in all life, and we learn to navigate our lives with wisdom, compassion, and grace.

This chapter has laid the foundation for our exploration of the Divine Feminine. As we move forward, we will delve deeper into the various aspects of the Divine Feminine and discover practical ways to integrate this powerful energy into our everyday lives.

So, dear reader, are you ready to awaken the Goddess within?

Feminine Energy: The Untold Power

The Role of Feminine Energy in Personal Growth

Picture a tree. It starts as a seed, buried beneath the earth, surrounded by darkness. Yet, within this tiny seed lies the potential for extraordinary growth. Given time, it sprouts roots, breaking through the soil to reach for the sunlight. In due course, this seed transforms into a majestic tree, standing tall, providing shade and bearing fruit. This process of transformation, of growth, mirrors the untold power of feminine energy within us.

Feminine energy is intimately tied to personal growth. It fuels our capacity to change, evolve, and flourish. It steers us to look inward, prompting us to question, to reflect, and to seek understanding. It encourages us to honor our feelings, to listen to our intuition, and to trust our inner wisdom. By doing so, we cultivate self-awareness, a crucial step in personal discovery and exploration.

Feminine energy also empowers us to be authentic. It prompts us to shed societal masks, to embrace our uniqueness, and to honor our truth. It champions self-love and self-acceptance, teaching us to value ourselves, not for what we do or what we have, but for who we are. By learning to love and accept ourselves, we build self-esteem and confidence, key ingredients for personal evolution.

Feminine Energy in Relationships

Think of a beautiful dance. Two partners, moving in harmony, their steps perfectly synchronized. They respond to each other's movements, their bodies communicating in a language beyond words. With every step, and every turn, they create a breathtaking display of unity and balance. This dance, in all its beauty and elegance, is a metaphor for the role of feminine energy in relationships.

Feminine energy fosters deep, meaningful connections. It enables us to empathize, to understand, and to care. It guides us to be open, receptive, and responsive to the feelings and needs of others. By doing so, it nurtures love, trust, and intimacy, strengthening the bonds of our relationships.

Yet, feminine energy is not just about nurturing others. It is also about nurturing ourselves. It reminds us to establish and maintain healthy boundaries, to honor our needs, and to practice self-care. It teaches us that self-love is not selfish but necessary and that we cannot pour from an empty cup. By taking care of ourselves, we ensure that we can show up as our best selves in our relationships.

Harnessing Feminine Energy for Emotional Healing

Imagine a river, its waters flowing smoothly, unhindered. Now if a dam is blocking the river, it causes the water to stagnate. Over time, the stagnant water becomes murky, losing its clarity and vitality. This imagery reflects our emotional landscape when we suppress our feelings, a practice often encouraged by a society that values stoicism over emotional expression. Yet, it is through the power of feminine energy that we can remove this dam and restore the flow of our emotions.

Feminine energy guides us toward emotional healing. It invites us to acknowledge our feelings, to honor them, and to express them in healthy ways. It allows us to cry when we are sad, to roar when we are angry, and to laugh and dance when we are happy. By doing so, it helps us to release suppressed emotions, cleanse our emotional landscape, and restore our emotional well-being.

Feminine energy also encourages us to be gentle with ourselves during this healing process. It reminds us that it is okay to feel, that it is okay to be vulnerable, and that it is okay to seek help when needed. It assures us that healing takes time, that it is okay to move at our own pace, and that it is okay to rest when we are tired. By embracing this gentle, compassionate approach, we create a safe space within us for healing to occur.

In essence, feminine energy is a powerful force for personal growth, relationship building, and emotional healing. It invites us to explore our depths, to celebrate our authenticity, and to express our emotions. It is a guide, a healer, and a nurturer. It is a source of strength, wisdom, and love. It is the very essence of our being, a sacred power that resides within us, waiting to be awakened and embraced.

The Divine Feminine: Not Just About Gender

Divine Feminine and the Spectrum of Gender

When we talk about the Divine Feminine, it's crucial to understand that it transcends the conventional concept of biological sex or gender. It's not an energy confined to women alone. Rather, it's a universal energy, a dimension of the psyche, a spiritual concept that exists within everyone, regardless of gender identity.

Think about a prism. When white light enters a prism, it disseminates into a spectrum of colors, each unique, yet all originating from the same source. Similarly, the human experience of gender is diverse, unique, and colorful, with every manifestation being a valid expression of the Divine Feminine.

The Divine Feminine is about receptivity, intuition, creativity, compassion, nurturing, and collaboration. These qualities are not exclusive to women. They can be found in men and non-binary individuals as well. When we limit the Divine Feminine to women, we inadvertently perpetuate gender stereotypes, restricting the full expression of this universal energy.

Divine Feminine in Men

In the context of men, the Divine Feminine manifests as the ability to be vulnerable, to express emotions, to empathize with others, and to nurture. It's the instinct to protect, to care, to create, and to collaborate. It's the capacity to listen, to understand, to be patient, and to love deeply. It's the wisdom that recognizes the strength in gentleness, the power in compassion, and the courage in vulnerability.

Consider two sides of the same coin. One side alone doesn't define the value of the coin. Similarly, the Divine Feminine and Divine Masculine are complementary energies, both required for a balanced and fulfilling life. For men, embracing the Divine Feminine is not about rejecting their masculinity but about finding a harmonious balance between the two energies. It's about acknowledging that being strong doesn't mean being unfeeling, that being brave doesn't mean being unyielding, and that being a man doesn't mean being devoid of compassion or tenderness.

Divine Feminine and Non-Binary Individuals

In the case of non-binary individuals, those who don't identify strictly as men or women, the Divine Feminine is an affirmation of their intrinsic value and validity. It's a testament to the diversity and fluidity of human experience.

The Divine Feminine is an acknowledgement that the divine isn't confined to binary gender norms, but is as diverse, fluid, and expansive as the universe itself. It's a validation of non-binary experiences, assuring them that they too are reflections of the divine, their identities a beautiful expression of the Divine Feminine.

Embracing the Divine Feminine allows non-binary individuals to connect with their intuition, to honor their emotions, to express their creativity, and to nurture their authentic selves. It's about recognizing that they too embody the sacred, that they too are bearers of the divine light.

In essence, the Divine Feminine is a celebration of diversity, a recognition of the multifaceted nature of the human experience. It's an invitation to honor our unique expression of divinity, to embody our authentic selves, to nurture our inherent worth, and to celebrate the sacred within us. It's a call to acknowledge that the divine is not confined to a particular gender or sex, but is the birthright of every soul, a universal energy that resides within us all.

Femininity Beyond Stereotypes

The notion of femininity is often wrapped in layers of societal expectations and stereotypes. We have been fed images of what it means to be feminine - delicate, gentle, nurturing, submissive. While these qualities are part of the feminine spectrum, they are not the entirety of it. The Divine Feminine invites us to challenge these stereotypes and expand our understanding of femininity.

Challenging Societal Views of Femininity

Femininity is not a one-size-fits-all concept. It is as diverse and unique as the women who embody it. Yet, society often presents us with a narrow, homogenized image of femininity. This image is insidiously pervasive, seeping into our consciousness, shaping our self-perception, and influencing our behavior.

The Divine Feminine calls us to question these societal views. It encourages us to challenge the idea that femininity is synonymous with weakness, that it is defined by our physical appearance, or that it is confined to certain roles or behaviors. It urges us to examine the limiting beliefs we may have internalized about our femininity and to dismantle them.

The Divine Feminine asks us to redefine femininity on our own terms. It invites us to explore what femininity means to us personally, to embrace our unique expression of it, and to honor the diverse expressions of femininity in others.

Femininity and Strength

Society often equates femininity with fragility and passivity. However, the Divine Feminine reminds us that there is immense strength in femininity. It is the strength of the ocean, powerful and deep, capable of nurturing life and reshaping landscapes. It is the strength of the earth, patient and enduring, bearing the weight of the world with grace.

Feminine strength is not loud or aggressive. It is quiet, subtle, and resilient. It is the strength of a tree bending in the wind, yielding yet unbroken. It is the strength of a river, flowing around obstacles, carving its path with patience and persistence.

Feminine strength is also the courage to be vulnerable, to open our hearts, and to express our emotions. It is the power to stand in our truth, to advocate for ourselves, and to set boundaries. It is the tenacity to face challenges, to overcome adversity, to rise from the ashes.

The Divine Feminine invites us to reclaim this strength. It encourages us to recognize the power within us, to celebrate our resilience, to honor our courage.

Femininity and Independence

Contrary to the traditional view that femininity is dependent and submissive, the Divine Feminine embodies independence and autonomy. It represents the freedom to make our own choices, to follow our own path, and to live according to our own values.

Feminine independence is about self-reliance. It is the ability to take care of ourselves, to meet our own needs, to advocate for our own well-being. It is the autonomy to make decisions about our bodies, our careers, our relationships, and our lives.

Feminine independence is also about mental and emotional freedom. It is the liberation from societal norms, expectations, and judgments. It is the freedom to be ourselves, to express our individuality, to embrace our uniqueness.

The Divine Feminine encourages us to cultivate this independence. It guides us to trust our intuition, to listen to our inner voice, and to honor our desires. It reminds us that we are the authors of our own story, the architects of our own destiny.

In conclusion, the Divine Feminine invites us to expand our understanding of femininity, to challenge societal stereotypes, to reclaim our strength, and to cultivate our independence. It encourages us to honor the multiplicity of femininity, to celebrate the diversity of feminine expressions, and to embody our unique version of femininity.

Through the lens of the Divine Feminine, we see that femininity is not a rigid mold that we must fit into, but a fluid spectrum that we can explore and express in our own unique way. We realize that femininity is not a limitation, but a source of strength, power, and freedom.

As we close this chapter, let us carry forward this expanded understanding of femininity. Let it inspire us to embrace our feminine energy, to embody the Divine Feminine, and to celebrate the sacredness of being a woman. Let it empower us to be our authentic selves, to live our truth, and to shine our light brightly.

Chapter Two

Embracing Your Feminine Energy

Have you ever gazed upon the clear night sky, with twinkling stars, and experienced a profound sense of vastness? In that moment, you were likely aware of a profound connection with nature, a sense of belonging to something much larger than yourself. This connection, this feeling of unity and oneness, is a powerful gateway to reconnecting with your inner Goddess, the divine feminine energy that resides within you.

The process of reconnecting with your inner Goddess is not a linear one. It is not a checklist to be completed or a race to be won. It is a deeply personal and transformative journey that unfolds in its own time and in its own unique way. It is a journey that invites you to look inward, to explore your depths, to honor your emotions, and to embrace your vulnerability. It is a journey that leads you to a deeper understanding and appreciation of yourself as a woman, as a divine being, as a manifestation of the Goddess.

Reconnecting with Your Inner Goddess

Self-Reflection Exercises

Reconnecting with your inner Goddess begins with self-reflection. It involves turning your gaze inward and listening to that inner voice. It requires you to tune into your feelings, your desires, your dreams, and your fears. It encourages you to question your beliefs, to confront your limitations, and to explore your potential.

One effective self-reflection exercise involves journaling. Set aside a few minutes each day to write in your journal. I will be honest, I write, but I find voicing it out works better for me. Whatever mode that resonates, let your thoughts flow freely, without judgment or censorship. Write about your feelings, your experiences, your hopes, and your challenges. As you put pen to paper, you may find insights and understandings emerging from the depths of your subconscious. You could also voice it out on a recording app and listen back. Some people may discover verbalizing flows more freely than writing.

Another powerful self-reflection exercise is meditation. Find a quiet space where you can sit or lie down comfortably. Close your eyes, take a few slow, deep breaths, and focus your attention inward. Observe your thoughts and feelings without attachment or judgment. Let them come and go, like clouds drifting across the sky. As you cultivate this practice of mindfulness, you begin to connect with your inner Goddess, the divine essence of your being.

Another way to meditate is through movement.

Meditation While Walking:

Walking meditation, often practiced in various contemplative traditions like Buddhism, involves bringing mindfulness to the act of walking. Instead of focusing on the breath as in seated meditation, attention is directed towards the sensations of walking itself. Here's how you might approach it:

1. **Mindful Steps**: Begin by standing still, grounding yourself, and then taking a few moments to become aware of your body and breath.

2. **Movement with Awareness**: As you start to walk, pay attention to the sensations in your feet as they lift, move, and touch the ground. Notice the shifting of weight, the muscles engaged, and the rhythm of your steps.

3. **Engage the Senses**: Expand your awareness to include other sensory experiences, such as the sights, sounds, and smells around you. Stay present with each moment as it unfolds.

4. **Return to the Present**: If your mind starts to wander, gently bring your attention back to the physical sensations of walking. Let go of any judgments or distractions, and simply be with each step.

Meditation While Dancing:

Dance meditation is a dynamic practice that encourages free expression and embodied awareness. It's about moving with intention, allowing the body to become a vehicle for meditation and self-expression. This is my daily practice! Here's how you might approach it:

1. **Connect with the Body**: Start by tuning into your body and its natural rhythms. Allow yourself to feel grounded and centered.

2. **Free Movement**: Begin to move freely, without any set choreography or expectations. Let the body lead, allowing movements to arise spontaneously.

3. **Expressive Flow**: Use dance as a means of expressing your innermost thoughts, feelings, and emotions. Allow the music to guide you, but also listen to the wisdom of your body.

4. **Mindful Presence**: Stay present with each movement, noticing the sensations, thoughts, and emotions that arise. Allow yourself to fully experience the dance in the present moment.

5. **Integration**: After your dance meditation, take a few moments to reflect on your experience. Notice any shifts in awareness or insights that may have emerged during the practice.

Whether you choose to practice walking meditation or dance meditation, both offer powerful opportunities for cultivating mindfulness, self-awareness, and inner peace. They invite us to connect with the present moment in a deeply embodied way, fostering a sense of harmony and wholeness within ourselves and the world around us.

Nature Immersion Activities

Nature is a beautiful mirror of the divine feminine. It reflects the cycles of birth, growth, decay, and renewal. It embodies the qualities of nurturing, receptivity, and creativity. By immersing ourselves in nature, we can attune to these qualities and awaken the Goddess within us.

Spend time outdoors whenever you can. Walk barefoot on the grass, feel the wind in your hair, listen to the birdsong. Notice the beauty and diversity of nature, from the tiny ant to the majestic tree. As you engage with nature in this way, you begin to feel a sense of kinship, a sense of interconnectedness that nurtures your inner Goddess.

Try practicing yoga or meditation in a natural setting. The sounds, smells, and textures of nature can enhance your practice, making it a more sensory and immersive experience. As you move your body or still your mind in the presence of nature, you create a sacred space for your inner Goddess to emerge.

Artistic Expression Techniques

Artistic expression is a powerful tool for reconnecting with your inner Goddess. It allows you to tap into your creativity, one of the core aspects of the divine feminine. It provides a medium for you to express your feelings, experiences, and insights in a tangible and meaningful way.

Experiment with different forms of artistic expression. It could be painting, dancing, writing, pottery, or any other art form that resonates with you. Don't worry about creating a masterpiece. The aim here is not to produce a work of art, but to express your inner self, to unleash your creativity, and to connect with your inner Goddess. Remember that the creative process is for you. Try not to let fear of judgment or criticism stop you from creating before you start.

For instance, you could try intuitive painting. This involves painting without a preconceived plan or design. You simply pick up a brush, choose your colors, and let your intuition guide your strokes. As you surrender to the process, you may find images, symbols, or patterns emerging on the canvas, revealing insights and messages from your inner Goddess.

On a personal level, I engage in dance every day, in one form or another. Embracing this as a morning ritual, I find solace in selecting my favorite tune and surrendering to the rhythm. This ritual is solely for personal enrichment, allowing the release of pent-up energy and emotions. Remarkably, just a brief five minutes of ecstatic movement can profoundly uplift one's energy levels.

Reconnecting with your inner Goddess involves a process of self-reflection, nature immersion, and artistic expression. It invites you to look inward, to explore your depths, and to express your unique essence. It empowers you to honor your feelings, to embrace your creativity, and to celebrate your divine femininity. Through this process, you awaken to the Goddess within, the sacred embodiment of your feminine energy.

The Path to Self-Love and Acceptance

Imagine for a moment that you are standing in front of a mirror, your reflection staring back at you. What do you see? How do you feel? For many of us, this exercise can bring up feelings of unease, judgment, and self-criticism. Yet, the path to embodying the Divine Feminine, to awakening the Goddess within, starts with a radical act of self-love and acceptance.

Affirmations for Self-Love

Have you ever noticed the inner dialogue that constantly plays in your mind? This internal chatter can often be negative, reinforcing self-doubt and insecurities. One powerful way to shift this narrative is through the use of affirmations. These are positive statements that, when repeated consistently, can help to reprogram our subconscious mind and foster self-love.

Louise L. Hay was a pioneering figure in the field of self-help and personal development, renowned for her groundbreaking work in empowering individuals to transform their lives through the power of positive affirmations. One of her most influential techniques, known as mirror work, has touched the lives of countless people seeking inner healing and self-love.

Through mirror work, Louise encouraged individuals to affirm their worthiness, embrace self-love, and cultivate a deeper sense of acceptance and compassion towards themselves. The affirmations used in mirror work are carefully crafted to instill positive beliefs and affirmations about oneself, such as "I am worthy," "I am deserving of love," and "I am enough." Speak these words with conviction and sincerity, feeling their resonance within you. Over time, you will notice a shift in your self-perception, a blossoming of self-love and self-respect.

The practice of mirror work is not merely about reciting affirmations mechanically but about fostering a genuine connection with oneself. It requires vulnerability, honesty, and a willingness to confront any inner resistance or self-doubt. Over time, consistent practice of mirror work can lead to profound shifts in self-perception, promoting greater self-esteem, confidence, and overall well-being.

Louise L. Hay's mirror work has resonated deeply with me to break free from negative thought patterns, heal emotional wounds, and cultivate a more loving relationship with myself.

Self-Care Practices

In our fast-paced, achievement-oriented society, it's easy to neglect our own needs in favor of fulfilling external demands and expectations. However, honoring the Divine Feminine within us requires that we prioritize self-care. This isn't about indulgence or vanity. Instead, it's about recognizing that we deserve to be nurtured and taken care of, not just by others, but by ourselves.

Establish a daily routine that includes activities that nourish your body, mind, and spirit. This could involve physical exercise, a balanced diet, sufficient rest, and activities that you enjoy and that bring you peace and happiness. It could also involve setting boundaries to protect your time and energy, saying no when necessary, and asking for help when you need it.

While the concept of self-care has gained widespread recognition in recent years, many individuals still struggle to prioritize it in their lives, often due to a lack of understanding or guidance on how to engage in effective self-care practices.

It's important to acknowledge that self-care isn't always intuitive, especially for those who haven't been taught how to prioritize their own needs or manage their well-being effectively. Factors such as upbringing, societal expectations, and personal experiences can influence our perceptions and attitudes towards self-care.

In some cases, individuals may find themselves grappling with challenges that hinder their ability to engage in self-care, such as mental health issues, trauma, or chronic stress. In such instances, seeking professional help can be instrumental in learning how to cultivate self-care practices that are meaningful and sustainable.

Therapists, counselors, and other mental health professionals can provide valuable guidance and support in exploring self-care strategies tailored to individual needs and circumstances. Through therapy or counseling sessions, individuals can gain insight into the underlying factors that may be impacting their ability to care for themselves effectively.

Additionally, mental health professionals can teach practical skills and techniques for managing stress, setting boundaries, practicing self-compassion, and enhancing overall well-being. They can also offer a safe space for individuals to explore their feelings, address any barriers to self-care, and develop personalized self-care plans.

It's essential to recognize that seeking professional help for self-care doesn't signify weakness or inadequacy but rather demonstrates a commitment to one's own growth and healing. Just as we seek guidance from experts in other areas of our lives, such as physical health or career development, seeking support for self-care is a proactive step towards cultivating a fulfilling and balanced life. I worked with different therapists and counselors at different points in my life and each one of them taught me something and helped me pivot.

Techniques for Self-Acceptance

Alongside self-love, self-acceptance is a fundamental step in embodying the Divine Feminine. Yet, accepting ourselves, with all our strengths and weaknesses, successes and failures, achievements and mistakes, can be challenging. It requires us to let go of the desire for perfection, to forgive ourselves for past mistakes, and to embrace our flaws as part of our unique beauty.

One technique to foster self-acceptance is to practice mindfulness. Mindfulness encourages us to be present and accepting of our current experience, without judgment or resistance. Through mindfulness, we learn to view ourselves with compassion and understanding, acknowledging our imperfections as natural and human.

Another technique is to challenge negative self-beliefs. We often hold onto limiting beliefs about ourselves that have been formed through past experiences or societal conditioning. By identifying and questioning these beliefs, we can start to dismantle them and replace them with more positive and empowering beliefs. This may sound really simple, but when I identify a negative self-limiting belief that seems to be rooted deeply – I will literally say "Stop it!" Sometimes you just have to shut the door and say "Enough!"

Remember, accepting yourself doesn't mean resigning yourself to stagnation. Rather, it means acknowledging where you are right now, recognizing that you are a work in progress, and giving yourself the grace and compassion to grow and evolve at your own pace. In this way, self-acceptance becomes the foundation for self-improvement, allowing you to embark on your path of personal growth from a place of love and kindness toward yourself.

As you explore the path to self-love and acceptance, remember this: You are a beautiful manifestation of the Divine Feminine. You are a beacon of love, wisdom, and power. You are deserving of love, respect, and kindness, especially from yourself. So, hold yourself with tenderness, cherish your unique beauty, and love yourself deeply. For in doing so, you are not only honoring the Goddess within you but are also radiating that divine love out into the world.

The Power of Vulnerability

Understanding the Strength in Vulnerability

Through my own authentic unfolding and being visible in the online space, someone asked me "Why be so vulnerable?"

Vulnerability, though often perceived as a weakness, is in reality a strength. It requires courage to open ourselves up, to expose our true selves, to risk criticism or rejection. Yet, it is through this openness, this willingness to be seen, that we connect with our authentic selves and with others on a deeper level.

I was once questioned about my choice to be open and vulnerable online. The reality is that pushing myself beyond my comfort zone, defying the constraints of my mind, and casting aside concerns, has proven to be one of the most liberating chapters in my life. Expressing my feminine sensuality in the digital realm fuels my creative spirit, nourishes my soul, and has profoundly shaped my sense of self. I acknowledge and embrace the fact that not everyone will appreciate me, while some will genuinely connect with and love me. Understanding that I can authentically be myself without seeking universal approval has allowed me to blossom into my truest self with increasing confidence and authenticity.

Vulnerability is an inherent part of the human experience. It is present in our moments of joy and pain, triumph and defeat, certainty and doubt. It is the thread that weaves together our shared experiences, bridging the gap between our individual worlds.

The Divine Feminine calls us to embrace our vulnerability. It invites us to honor our feelings, to express our needs, to show our true selves. It encourages us to let go of the armor we wear to protect ourselves, to drop the masks we put on to fit in, to step out of the shadows and into the light.

The strength in vulnerability lies not in resistance, but in surrender. Not in hiding, but in revealing. Not in hardness, but in softness. It is the strength of a flower blooming in the wild, of a river flowing around a rock, of a bird taking flight. It is the strength that comes from being real, from being human, from being you.

Exercises for Embracing Vulnerability

Often, the first step towards embracing vulnerability is acknowledging our fears and reservations about it. This can be achieved through mindfulness and reflection. Pay attention to situations where you feel vulnerable. What emotions do you experience? What thoughts run through your mind? What physical sensations do you notice in your body? Observing these responses can give you insights into your relationship with vulnerability.

Another way to cultivate vulnerability is through authenticity. Practice expressing your thoughts and feelings honestly, without filtering or censoring them. Speak your truth, even when it's uncomfortable or inconvenient. Show up as your authentic self, even when it's scary or risky.

Remember, embracing vulnerability is not about being reckless or oversharing. It's about discerning when to open up and to whom. It's about trusting your intuition to guide you toward safe and supportive environments where you can express your vulnerability without fear of harm or judgment.

Practice vulnerability in small, manageable steps. It could be as simple as sharing your feelings with a trusted friend, asking for help when you need it, or admitting when you don't know something. Each small act of vulnerability strengthens your courage and confidence, empowering you to embrace vulnerability in bigger and more challenging situations.

Vulnerability in Relationships

Think of vulnerability as the key that opens the door to deeper connections. In relationships, vulnerability allows us to be seen and understood, to share our joys and sorrows, our dreams and fears, our strengths and weaknesses. It creates a space for empathy, for intimacy, for love to flourish.

In a relationship, expressing vulnerability could mean sharing your feelings honestly, admitting when you're wrong, or revealing your insecurities. It could mean standing up for your needs, setting boundaries, or asking for what you want. It could mean showing your affection, your admiration, or your gratitude openly and sincerely.

Remember, vulnerability is a two-way street. It involves not only expressing your own vulnerability but also responding to the vulnerability of others with empathy and compassion. When someone opens up to you, listen with an open heart and an open mind. Offer your understanding, your support, your love. By doing so, you create a safe space for vulnerability, a space where both of you can be your authentic selves.

The Divine Feminine invites us to embrace vulnerability as a strength, a gift, a bridge to deeper connections. It encourages us to open our hearts, to reveal our true selves, to let our light shine. In the dance of life, vulnerability is not a stumbling step, but a graceful leap, a powerful twirl, a beautiful expression of our human spirit. So, dance with vulnerability, dance with life, dance with the Divine Feminine within you. Let your vulnerability be your strength, your authenticity be your guide, and your heart be your compass.

Nurturing Your Femininity

Femininity is like a precious seed; it holds within itself the potential for extraordinary growth and blossoming. Yet, like any seed, it needs to be tenderly cared for and nurtured. It needs to be watered with love, nourished with respect, and bathed in the light of self-acceptance. Here are some ways to cultivate and nourish your femininity.

Daily Rituals for Honoring Femininity

The rhythm of our daily lives can often feel fast-paced and hectic, leaving us little time to connect with our feminine energy. However, integrating small rituals into our daily routine can provide gentle reminders to honor and embrace our femininity.

One such ritual can be as simple as savoring a cup of herbal tea or coffee in the morning. As you prepare the drink, take a moment to appreciate the aroma, the warmth, the flavor. Let the act of drinking be a mindful experience, a moment of stillness in your day, a time to nourish your body and honor your feminine energy.

Another ritual could be setting aside a few minutes each day for a self-massage. Using essential oils like lavender or rose, gently massage your hands, feet, or any part of your body that you feel needs care. This not only helps to relax and rejuvenate your body, but also serves as a tangible reminder of self-love and self-care, key aspects of feminine energy.

Feminine Wardrobe and Style Tips

Our clothes are an external expression of our inner selves. They're a way to communicate our identity and how we feel about ourselves. Therefore, cultivating a wardrobe that resonates with your feminine energy can be a powerful way to nurture your femininity.

Start by choosing clothes that make you feel beautiful and comfortable. These could be dresses that flow gracefully around your body, blouses in soft, warm colors, or accessories that add a touch of elegance and charm. Remember, the goal is not to conform to societal standards of beauty or femininity, but to express your unique style and personality.

When it comes to makeup, less is often more. Embrace your natural beauty and use makeup to enhance, rather than mask, your features. A light touch of mascara to highlight your eyes, a sweep of blush to add a healthy glow to your cheeks, and a dab of lip balm to keep your lips soft and hydrated can make you feel feminine and beautiful.

Feminine Energy Foods

What we eat has a profound impact on our physical health and our overall energy. Certain foods are known to nourish our feminine energy, supporting our hormonal balance, enhancing our mood, and promoting our wellbeing.

Dark leafy greens like spinach, kale, and collard greens are packed with nutrients that support feminine health. They are rich in iron, calcium, and magnesium, which are essential for maintaining hormonal balance and supporting reproductive health.

Berries are another great food for nurturing feminine energy. They are rich in antioxidants and vitamin C, which boost immunity and enhance skin health. Plus, their sweet taste and vibrant colors can uplift your mood and tickle your senses.

Foods rich in healthy fats, like avocados, nuts, and seeds, are also beneficial for feminine health. They provide essential fatty acids that support hormonal balance, promote healthy skin, and enhance mood.

In essence, nurturing your femininity involves cultivating daily rituals that honor your feminine energy, expressing your unique style through your wardrobe, and nourishing your body with feminine energy foods. These practices serve as touchstones, gently guiding you back to your feminine essence, reminding you of the divine feminine energy that flows through you, and inviting you to honor and embrace it in every aspect of your life.

As we turn the page, let's carry this sense of nurturing and embracing our femininity into the next chapter, where we dive into the fascinating world of divine feminine archetypes. Just as a diamond has many facets, so does the divine feminine, and it's time to explore and celebrate each and every one of them.

Chapter Three

Archetypes of the Divine Feminine

Estimates suggest there are hundreds of thousands of different species of flowering plants worldwide. It's safe to say that there are a vast number of different flowers, each with its own unique beauty and characteristics. Similarly, the Divine Feminine is not a singular entity but a spectrum of varying energies and characteristics. Embedded within this spectrum are the archetypes: universally recognized symbols or themes that embody specific aspects of the Divine Feminine. They are the flowers in the garden of the Divine Feminine, each with its unique beauty and significance.

The exploration of these archetypes can serve as a valuable tool for personal growth, self-understanding, and spiritual development. By identifying with different archetypes, we can tap into their unique energies, embody their qualities, and integrate their wisdom into our daily lives. The truth is you may identify with one archetype more than others, which could indicate an imbalance. Understanding all of the archetypes can help highlight where you could balance the scales. For example, this chapter will be starting with the Mother archetype. Personally, this is one that I am highly identified with being a single mom of two children. When I allowed myself to access my Wise Woman, however, I started to play with the Maiden archetype who loves to play, and the Lover archetype which is all about engaging in pleasure and sensuality.

The Mother: The Nurturer

Understanding the Mother Archetype

Picture a warm embrace, a soothing lullaby, a comforting bowl of soup on a cold day. These are all expressions of the Mother archetype, the embodiment of nurturing, caring, and unconditional love. Rooted in our biological experience of motherhood, this archetype extends beyond the literal act of giving birth or having children. It represents our capacity to nurture and care for others, to provide comfort and support, and to foster growth and development.

The Mother archetype is associated with qualities such as compassion, patience, generosity, and understanding. She is the giver of life, the nurturer of dreams, the healer of wounds. She is the safe haven we return to in times of distress, the guiding light that leads us through the darkness.

Yet, the Mother archetype is not confined to women or mothers. It is a universal energy that can be embodied by anyone, regardless of gender or parental status. It is the nurturing love we show to ourselves, the care we extend to our loved ones, the support we offer to our community.

Embodying the Mother Archetype

Embodying the Mother archetype involves cultivating a nurturing, caring, and compassionate attitude towards ourselves and others. It's about being kind to ourselves, taking care of our physical, emotional, and spiritual needs, and treating ourselves with love and respect.

To nurture others, we can start by offering a listening ear, a shoulder to lean on, or a word of encouragement. We can show our care through simple acts of kindness, such as preparing a meal for a loved one, sending a thoughtful message to a friend, or volunteering in our community.

Practicing mindfulness can also help us embody the Mother archetype. By being present and attentive, we can tune into the needs of ourselves and others, respond with empathy and understanding, and provide the right kind of support at the right time.

The Mother Archetype in Daily Life

In daily life, the Mother archetype can manifest in various ways. At home, it might look like creating a warm and welcoming environment, preparing nutritious meals, or caring for a sick family member. At work, it could be mentoring a junior colleague, facilitating a team project, or leading with empathy and collaboration.

As a friend or community member, embodying the Mother archetype could mean offering emotional support, volunteering for a local charity, or advocating for those who are vulnerable or marginalized.

In self-care, the Mother archetype encourages us to nurture our wellbeing, to rest when we are tired, to nourish ourselves with healthy food, to engage in activities that bring us joy and relaxation.

By embodying the Mother archetype, we connect with our capacity for nurturing, caring, and loving. We cultivate a compassionate heart, an understanding mind, and a generous spirit. We become a source of comfort, support, and growth for ourselves and those around us.

As we journey through life, let the Mother archetype be our guide. Let it inspire us to nurture, to care, to love. Let it remind us of our innate capacity for compassion, generosity, and understanding. Let it encourage us to create a world filled with kindness, empathy, and mutual support. This is the essence of the Mother archetype, the embodiment of the nurturing spirit of the Divine Feminine.

The Warrior: The Protector

Understanding the Warrior Archetype

There's a formidable force within each of us, a force that stands tall in the face of adversity, fights for justice, and protects what is precious. This force, dear readers, is encapsulated in the Warrior archetype. This aspect of the Divine Feminine is not about aggression or violence. Instead, it symbolizes inner strength, courage, and resilience.

The Warrior archetype is a guardian, standing at the boundaries of our selfhood, warding off external influences that seek to shape us into something we're not. It's the voice inside us that speaks up when our values are compromised, the resolve that keeps us moving forward when obstacles arise.

The Warrior within us is the embodiment of conviction, the unyielding belief in our worth, abilities, and dreams. It's the fiery spirit that refuses to be extinguished, the spark that ignites change and transformation.

Embodying the Warrior Archetype

Embracing the Warrior archetype is about recognizing our inner strength and courage. It's about standing up for ourselves and our beliefs, setting healthy boundaries, and asserting our needs and desires.

To embody the Warrior, we must first acknowledge our personal power. We can do this by reflecting on our past victories - the challenges we've overcome, the changes we've initiated, the battles we've won. These reflections serve as reminders of our strength and resilience, fueling our confidence and courage.

Next, we must cultivate a positive mindset. The Warrior within us thrives on positivity, resilience, and determination. We can nurture these attributes by monitoring our thoughts, pruning out the negative, false thoughts and reframing, and celebrating our accomplishments, no matter how small.

Embodying the Warrior also involves developing courage. Courage is not the absence of fear, but the willingness to act despite it. We can cultivate courage by stepping out of our comfort zone, taking risks, and facing our fears head-on.

Each courageous act, no matter how small, strengthens our inner Warrior, empowering us to tackle bigger challenges.

Lastly, the Warrior archetype teaches us about protection - not just physical protection, but emotional and spiritual protection as well. It's about guarding our energy, maintaining our emotional balance, and protecting our spiritual wellbeing. We can do this by setting clear boundaries, practicing self-care, and nurturing our inner peace.

The Warrior Archetype in Daily Life

In our daily life, the Warrior archetype can manifest in various ways. In our personal relationships, it may show up as the courage to express our feelings, the strength to assert our needs, or the determination to protect our boundaries. I often recognize this as anger. Anger can be a catalyst for action. It's not about reacting from the anger, but using it to create change.

In our professional life, the Warrior can be the driving force that propels us towards our goals, the resilience that keeps us going in the face of obstacles, and the conviction that inspires us to stand up for our values.

When facing challenges, the Warrior within us provides the strength to persevere, the tenacity to keep going, and the courage to confront and overcome our fears.

In our personal growth journey, the Warrior archetype is the catalyst for change, the spark that ignites transformation. It's the resolve that fuels our commitment to growth, the courage that enables us to face our shadows, and the strength that empowers us to make positive changes in our lives.

The Warrior archetype reminds us that we are stronger than we think, braver than we believe, and more powerful than we realize. It's the fire within us, the flame that can light the way in the darkest of times, the beacon that can guide us to our true potential.

As we navigate the path of life, let us draw upon the strength of the Warrior, the courage of the protector, and the resilience of the fighter. Let us stand tall in the face of adversity, let our voices be heard, let our light shine bright. This is the essence of the Warrior archetype, a testament to the formidable strength and courage of the Divine Feminine within us.

The Wise Woman: The Guide

Understanding the Wise Woman Archetype

Think of a well-worn book, its pages filled with age-old wisdom. Or perhaps an ancient tree, standing tall and rooted, bearing the wisdom of ages in its rings. These images capture the essence of the Wise Woman archetype, an embodiment of the Divine Feminine that represents wisdom, intuition, and guidance.

The Wise Woman is not defined by chronological age, but by the depth of her understanding and insight. She is the voice of intuition whispering in our ear, the gentle nudge that guides us towards our truth. She is the spark of creativity that inspires us, the wellspring of wisdom within us.

The Wise Woman holds a lantern, illuminating the path ahead and revealing the lessons hidden in our experiences. She sees beyond the surface, discerning the deeper meanings and connections in life. She values knowledge, but more importantly, she values understanding and wisdom, which come from introspection and life experience.

The Wise Woman archetype is a guide, a mentor, a counselor. She encourages us to listen to our inner voice, to trust our intuition, and to seek wisdom from within. She reminds us that every experience, every relationship, every challenge carries a lesson, a nugget of wisdom to be gleaned.

Embodying the Wise Woman Archetype

Embodying the Wise Woman archetype is a process of inner discovery and growth. It involves tapping into our inner wisdom, honing our intuition, and cultivating a deep sense of understanding and empathy.

To awaken the Wise Woman within, we need to cultivate stillness and introspection. We can do this through practices such as meditation, journaling, or simply spending quiet time in nature. These practices create a space for our inner wisdom to surface, for our intuitive insights to emerge.

Another key aspect of embodying the Wise Woman is embracing our life experiences as sources of wisdom. This involves viewing our past not as a series of random events, but as a rich tapestry of lessons and growth opportunities. It's about finding meaning in our experiences, extracting wisdom from our successes and failures, joys and sorrows.

Embodying the Wise Woman also involves nurturing our intuition. Intuition is our inner compass, guiding us towards our truth. We can strengthen our intuition by paying attention to our gut feelings, our hunches, our flashes of insight. Over time, we learn to trust our intuition, to heed its guidance, to honor its wisdom.

The Wise Woman Archetype in Daily Life

In our daily life, the Wise Woman archetype can guide us in many ways. It can help us make decisions that are aligned with our truth, navigate challenges with wisdom and grace, and cultivate deeper understanding and empathy in our relationships.

In decision-making, the Wise Woman within can guide us to make choices that reflect our deepest values and aspirations. Instead of being swayed by external influences, we learn to listen to our inner voice, to trust our intuition, to honor our truth.

In facing challenges, the Wise Woman can help us see the bigger picture, to find the lessons hidden in our struggles, to transform obstacles into opportunities for growth. Instead of resisting challenges, we learn to embrace them as stepping stones on our path to wisdom.

In our relationships, the Wise Woman archetype can guide us to cultivate understanding, empathy, and compassion. We learn to listen deeply, to understand different perspectives, to respond with wisdom and grace. Instead of reacting impulsively, we learn to respond mindfully, guided by our inner wisdom.

In essence, embodying the Wise Woman archetype is about awakening to our inner wisdom, trusting our intuition, and navigating life with understanding and grace. It's about honoring our life experiences as sources of wisdom, and using this wisdom to guide us on our path. As we embody the Wise Woman, we become our own guide, our own mentor, our own source of wisdom. We realize that the answers we seek are not out there, but within us, waiting to be discovered.

With the wisdom of the Wise Woman within us, we are equipped to navigate the complexities of life with grace, understanding, and insight. We are guided to make decisions that reflect our truth, to transform challenges into opportunities, and to cultivate deep understanding and empathy in our relationships. So, let the Wise Woman within guide you, illuminate your path, and awaken the wisdom that resides within you. Embody the Wise Woman, and let her wisdom be your guide.

The Lover: The Life-Giver

Understanding the Lover Archetype

Consider the radiant glow of a sunset, the intoxicating scent of a blooming rose, the soul-stirring melody of a love song. These sensual experiences evoke a sense of passion, pleasure, and connection, mirroring the energy of The Lover archetype. In the realm of Divine Feminine archetypes, The Lover represents sensuality, passion, and a deep emotional connection to self, others, and the world around.

Far from being solely about romantic love or physical attraction, The Lover archetype encompasses a broader spectrum of love. It's about a profound appreciation of beauty, a deep sense of empathy, and a rich emotional life. The

Lover savors every moment, seeks deep and meaningful connections, and passionately engages with life.

The Lover archetype is the source of our creativity, our joy, and our zest for life. It is the energy that fuels our passions, nourishes our relationships, and brings color to our world. It is the flame that lights up our hearts, the spark that sets our souls on fire, the intoxicating elixir that makes life worth living.

Embodying the Lover Archetype

Embodying The Lover archetype means awakening to the sensual, passionate, and emotional aspects of our being. It involves celebrating our senses, honoring our emotions, and passionately engaging with life.

Sensuality is a key aspect of The Lover archetype. It's about fully experiencing and savoring life through our senses - the sight of a beautiful landscape, the sound of a melodious tune, the taste of a delicious meal, the scent of fresh flowers, the touch of a loved one. Engaging in activities that stimulate our senses can help us connect with The Lover within us.

Emotions are the language of The Lover archetype. Embodying this archetype means allowing ourselves to feel deeply, to express our emotions freely, and to navigate life with emotional intelligence. It involves honoring our joy, our sadness, our anger, our fear, and our love. It's about living heartfully, not merely mindfully.

Lastly, passion is the lifeblood of The Lover archetype. To embody this archetype, we need to identify our passions and pursue them wholeheartedly. Whether it's a hobby, a cause, a dream, or a relationship, passionately engaging with what we love can ignite The Lover energy within us.

The Lover Archetype in Daily Life

The Lover archetype can manifest in various ways in our daily life. In our relationships, it can guide us to cultivate deep emotional connections, to express our feelings openly, and to create a nurturing and sensual environment. It can help us build relationships that are not just about companionship, but also about mutual growth, shared passion, and deep emotional bonding.

In our work, The Lover can inspire us to pursue what we love, to infuse passion into our tasks, and to create with joy and enthusiasm. It can help us transform our work from a mere means of livelihood into an expression of our passion, a manifestation of our love.

In our personal growth, The Lover archetype can guide us to honor our emotions, to cultivate emotional intelligence, and to live a passionate and fulfilling life. It can inspire us to explore our inner world, to face our shadows with love, and to transform our wounds into wisdom.

To sum up, The Lover archetype invites us to awaken to our sensuality, honor our emotions, and live our passions. It calls us to love deeply, live passionately, and savor every moment of our existence. It is the essence of love, the fountain of passion, the symphony of life. So, let us answer the call of The Lover, let us dance to the rhythm of love, let us savor the symphony of life.

The Maiden – The Ultimate Receiver

Understanding the Maiden Archetype

The Maiden archetype represents youthfulness, innocence, new beginnings, and the blossoming of potential. Often depicted as a young woman in her adolescence or early adulthood, the Maiden embodies qualities of purity, vitality, and curiosity. Embracing the Maiden archetype involves cultivating a sense of wonder, embracing new experiences, and nurturing the seeds of potential within oneself.

The Maiden symbolizes purity of heart and innocence of spirit. She approaches the world with an open mind and a childlike wonder, free from the burdens of past experiences or preconceived notions. The Maiden understands that her strength is in surrender. She embraces change with optimism and enthusiasm, eager to explore new horizons and embark on adventures. The

Maiden is endlessly curious about the world around her. She approaches life with a sense of exploration and discovery, seeking to learn and grow from every experience she encounters. She lives in the present moment and is carefree. She doesn't hold on to the past.

Embodying the Maiden Archetype

This is really about following your pleasure. It is taking a day off from your responsibilities and having fun. It could be revisiting childhood activities like drawing or dancing. It could be as simple as doing nothing and staring at the clouds. It may be dressing up extravagantly in costume. I always enjoyed this as a child and still love to dress up in costume and become a character.

Imagine the maiden as being different than what you would usually do. Take a different route, walk instead of drive. Where you may usually keep to yourself, be bold, and smile at a stranger. Could you give compliments to people?

The Maiden Archetype in Daily Life

In our daily lives, we can approach the day with a sense of openness and curiosity, welcoming new experiences and opportunities for growth. The maiden is willing to step outside of our comfort zones and explore unfamiliar territories, even though it's scary. This is the risk-taking archetype.

Cultivate your creative potential by engaging in activities that inspire and energize you. Whether it's painting, writing, dancing, or gardening, find outlets for self-expression that allow you to tap into your inner creativity.

Embrace the innocence and joy of the Maiden by cultivating a sense of playfulness and spontaneity in your daily life. Find moments of laughter and lightheartedness, and approach challenges with a sense of optimism and resilience.

With personal growth, we can embody the maiden by recognizing that life is a continuous cycle of beginnings and endings. It is finding joy in the simple pleasures of life, and letting your enthusiasm for living shine brightly for all to see.

By embodying the Maiden archetype, we can tap into our youthful vitality, creativity, and sense of wonder, and approach life with a fresh perspective and an open heart, ready to embrace all the beauty and magic the world offers.

The Queen – The Leader

Understanding the Divine Feminine Queen Archetype

The Divine Feminine Queen archetype represents sovereignty, power, grace, and wisdom. She embodies the essence of feminine leadership, ruling with compassion, strength, and integrity. Embracing the Divine Feminine Queen archetype involves recognizing and honoring the inherent worth and dignity of oneself and others, while also embracing one's capacity to lead and inspire positive change.

Embodying the Queen Archetype

Embodying the Queen archetype goes beyond simply holding a position of leadership; it entails stepping into your power with boldness and confidence, driven by a sense of purpose and a commitment to leaving a lasting impact. The Queen understands that she is part of something greater than herself and is dedicated to fulfilling her mission with determination and resilience.

The Queen is guided by a sense of purpose and a vision for the future. She understands that her actions have the potential to create meaningful change in the world and is committed to leaving a legacy that reflects her values and ideals. Identify your own mission or purpose and align your actions with this guiding principle.

While the Queen may be focused on her mission and career, she also finds fulfillment in nurturing long-term relationships. This may manifest in partnerships, friendships, or family connections that provide support, love, and companionship along the journey. Invest in building strong and meaningful relationships that nourish your soul and contribute to your overall sense of fulfillment.

The Queen Archetype in Daily Life

The queen archetype involves some self-reflection. Identify your personal strengths and values: What are you uniquely good at? What do you care about? What lights you up inside?

This is a good direction towards what your mission is. It can evolve and change but it's a commitment to discovering more and more of you.

This is also accessing your inner radiance royalty. Imagine standing up straight, shoulders back. Regal, proud, confident. Maybe it's even putting on red lipstick and high heels and making an entrance. Whatever it is – it's big and bold energy.

Remember to play with this energy if it's new to you. Make it fun and less serious. Be the Queen you are.

By embodying the Divine Feminine Queen archetype, you can tap into your own inner power, wisdom, and grace, and lead with compassion, strength, and integrity, inspiring positive change and transformation in the world around you.

The Wild Woman – The Force of Nature

Understanding the Wild Woman

I have become well acquainted with the wild woman especially when it comes to self-expression, creativity, and having a voice in the world. The wild woman challenges the status quo. She is not tied to family bonds. She doesn't fit in and she doesn't want to. She is a force of nature and is pure freedom.

The Wild Woman archetype was popularized by Clarissa Pinkola Estés in her book "Women Who Run With the Wolves," and represents the untamed, instinctual, and primal aspects of femininity. It's a concept that transcends gender boundaries, speaking to the raw, unbridled essence within all individuals. Embodying the Wild Woman archetype involves tapping into your primal instincts, reclaiming lost parts of yourself, and embracing your true nature without inhibition or apology.

Embodying the Wild Woman

The Wild Woman is deeply connected to her instincts and intuition. She trusts her inner guidance and doesn't conform to societal expectations that may suppress her innate wisdom. She is fiercely independent and resists being confined by societal norms or expectations. She embraces her autonomy and follows her own path, even if it means going against the grain.

Creativity flows freely through the Wild Woman. She expresses herself authentically and passionately, whether through art, dance, writing, or any other form of creative expression. She rejects conformity in favor of originality and innovation. The Wild Woman challenges oppressive systems and structures that seek to control or suppress her. She refuses to be constrained by limitations imposed by others and fights for her freedom and autonomy.

The Wild Woman Archetype in Daily Life

We can connect to the wild woman every day in various ways. Spending time in nature to reconnect with our primal instincts and tap into the wildness within. Tapping into the wild woman can look like engaging in activities such as hiking, camping, dancing naked, or simply immersing yourself in natural surroundings.

In our personal growth, we can cultivate our intuition by practicing listening to our intuition and trusting our gut feelings. When we learn to pay attention to the messages in our bodies that our emotions are sending us, we can then honor our inner guidance. It took me a long time to listen and trust my intuition. I have been in relationships where there were obvious red flags, and I chose not to listen to my gut feelings. However, I learned the value of my intuition from those exact experiences when I didn't listen to it.

In terms of relationships, release attachments to people, places, or things that no longer serve your highest good, and embrace the liberation that comes from living authentically and on your own terms.

The wild woman finds creative outlets to express herself freely and authentically. Whether it's through art, music, dance, or writing, let go of self-doubt and fear of judgment, and allow your true essence to shine through. Question societal norms and expectations that don't resonate with your true self. Be willing to stand apart from the crowd and forge your own path, even if it means facing resistance or criticism from observers.

This is not an easy path. Through my authentic expression online, I have faced harsh criticism. My art and expression is my sensuality and I express that through sensual and erotic dancing. At the root of it, I know why I do what I do – to express myself authentically. Having other people's understanding is not necessary.

By embodying the Wild Woman archetype, you can tap into your innate power, creativity, and authenticity, and live a life that is wild, free, and true to your deepest essence.

And with that, we close this exploration of the Divine Feminine archetypes. As we move forward, let us carry these insights in our hearts. Let us honor the Mother, the Warrior, the Wise Woman, the Lover, the Maiden, the Queen, and the Wild Woman within us. Let us celebrate the diversity and richness of the Divine Feminine. Above all, let us remember that we are, each and every one of us, a beautiful expression of the Divine Feminine, a unique manifestation of the Goddess.

Chapter Four

The Divine Balance: Feminine and Masculine Energies

A balanced fitness routine incorporates elements of strength training and endurance exercises (masculine) with activities like yoga or dance that focus on flexibility, grace, and inner connection (feminine).

The movements of strength training are vastly different from dance moves, yet together they create a solid foundation for a strong and graceful body that is harmonious and balanced. Such is the dance of energies within us - the interplay between the feminine and masculine aspects of our being.

It's important to note that when we speak of feminine and masculine energies, we're not talking strictly about genders, but rather, about complementary forces that exist within each of us, regardless of our gender identity. By understanding and harmonizing these energies, we can achieve a state of inner balance that significantly enhances our well-being and enriches our life experiences.

The Dance of Energies: Feminine vs Masculine

Understanding Feminine and Masculine Energies

Feminine and masculine energies are fundamental aspects of our psyche and consciousness. They represent two poles of our existence, two sides of the same coin, each bearing unique qualities and attributes.

Feminine energy is often associated with attributes such as intuition, compassion, creativity, empathy, and nurturing. It's the force that allows us to form deep connections, nurture ourselves and others, and tap into our creativity and intuition. Think of it as the soothing ebb of the ocean tide or the nurturing warmth of the earth.

On the other hand, masculine energy is typically linked to qualities such as assertiveness, logic, action, and independence. It's the force that drives us to take action, to assert ourselves, and to think logically. Picture it as the steady push of a river or the solid strength of a mountain.

The Interplay of Feminine and Masculine Energies

Just like a balanced relationship involves both partners contributing their strengths while also being receptive to each other's needs, our feminine and masculine energies are constantly in motion, each influencing and balancing the other. This dance of energies is not about one dominating the other; rather, it's about each energy complementing and harmonizing with the other to create a balanced inner landscape.

For instance, when we're faced with a problem, our masculine energy might prompt us to analyze the situation logically and devise a plan of action, while our feminine energy could guide us to consider the emotional aspects and the impact on others involved. By honoring both perspectives, we can arrive at a solution that is both practical and empathetic.

Feminine and Masculine Energies in Relationships

The balance of feminine and masculine energies is also crucial in our relationships. Whether it's a romantic partnership, a friendship, or a professional relationship, harmony between these energies can foster healthier and more fulfilling connections.

For example, in a romantic relationship, if one partner is embodying their masculine energy, taking charge of planning dates or making decisions, the other partner can balance that by stepping into their feminine energy, being open, receptive, and nurturing. However, it's important to allow for fluidity, giving each partner the freedom to express both their masculine and feminine energies as the situation demands and as they feel comfortable.

In friendships and professional relationships, this balance can manifest as a mutual respect for each other's ideas (masculine energy) and feelings (feminine energy), and a balance between giving advice (masculine energy) and offering emotional support (feminine energy).

Understanding and balancing our feminine and masculine energies is a transformative process. It's about acknowledging and honoring all aspects of our being. It's about inviting harmony and balance into our inner world, which inevitably reflects in our outer world. So, let's continue to explore this dance of energies and discover ways to nurture this balance in our everyday lives.

Embracing Your Inner Masculine

Understanding the Inner Masculine

The inner masculine is the part of our psyche that embodies qualities often associated with masculinity such as assertiveness, logic, and action. It's the part of us that stands up for our beliefs, takes decisive action, and employs logical thinking to solve problems.

The inner masculine is not about gender or sex, but rather about a type of energy that exists within all of us, regardless of our gender identity. It's the energy that pushes us to set and achieve our goals, to protect our boundaries, and to assert our individuality.

However, many of us, especially those who identify as female, have been conditioned to suppress our inner masculine. We've been told that being assertive is being bossy, that taking charge is controlling, and that expressing anger is being hysterical. This has led to an imbalance in our inner energies, often causing us to feel disempowered, disconnected, and unfulfilled.

In today's fast-paced world, many of us are indeed dominated by masculine energy, which emphasizes traits like rationality, logic, and productivity. While these qualities are valuable and necessary for achievement and success, an overemphasis on them can lead to imbalance and burnout.

Techniques for Embracing the Inner Masculine

To embrace our inner masculine, we need to start by acknowledging and appreciating its presence within us. Recognize the times when you've asserted yourself, when you've taken decisive action, when you've employed logical thinking to solve a problem. These are all expressions of your inner masculine. Be mindful throughout the day and notice where you are being rational about something. This can express itself as thinking, comparing, defending, or seeking evidence. Masculine energy shows up as figuring out "how" something may happen.

Next, challenge the societal conditioning that has led to the suppression of your inner masculine. Question the beliefs that assertiveness is bossiness, that taking charge is controlling, and that expressing anger is hysteria. Replace these limiting beliefs with empowering ones that honor and validate your inner masculine.

Exploring the dynamics of our relationships with the masculine figures in our lives is crucial for understanding and healing our own masculine energy. Whether it's our relationship with our father, spouse, brother, teachers, partners, past lovers, or sons, each connection offers insights into how we relate to masculine energy and how it influences us.

If there's trauma or unresolved issues stemming from these relationships, seeking support from a trained professional such as a counselor or therapist can provide a safe space to delve deeper into these experiences and work towards healing. They can offer guidance and techniques to navigate through any emotional wounds and facilitate the process of restoring balance and harmony within ourselves.

I've been mindful of how I engage with my son regarding his absent father, acknowledging and understanding my own emotions to better support him. Additionally, I've been vigilant about preventing any resentment towards his father from impacting our relationship unintentionally. Recognizing that these dynamics can operate subconsciously, I've proactively sought therapy at various points for guidance and healing through these emotional challenges.

Incorporating activities that stimulate the inner masculine can also be beneficial. This could include physical activities like running or weightlifting, mental activities like solving puzzles or strategizing, or creative activities like woodworking or playing a musical instrument. These activities not only provide an outlet for your inner masculine but also help to build confidence and resilience.

Lastly, practice standing up for yourself, asserting your needs, and setting healthy boundaries. These are all expressions of your inner masculine, and by practicing them, you strengthen and honor this aspect of your being.

Balancing the Inner Masculine with the Divine Feminine

While it's important to embrace our inner masculine, it's equally important to maintain balance with our divine feminine. The inner masculine and divine feminine are not opposing forces, but complementary ones. They work together, each bringing unique qualities and strengths to create a balanced and whole individual.

Finding a balance between these energies is a dynamic, ongoing process. It's not about achieving a perfect 50/50 balance, but about tuning into your needs and adjusting accordingly. There may be times when you need to tap more into your inner masculine, like when you need to make a difficult decision or stand up for yourself. At other times, you might need to connect more with your divine feminine, like when you need to nurture yourself or others, or when you need to tap into your intuition.

A balanced inner masculine and divine feminine can manifest as the ability to take decisive action with empathy, to assert ourselves while considering others' feelings, and to stand up for our beliefs while staying open to different perspectives. It's about integrating our strength with our sensitivity, our logic with our intuition, our action with our contemplation.

Embracing the inner masculine is an integral part of our journey toward wholeness and balance. It's about acknowledging and honoring our masculine energy, challenging societal conditioning, and finding balance with our divine feminine. By embracing our inner masculine, we reclaim our power, assert our individuality, and step into a more authentic and balanced version of ourselves.

Strategies for Harmonizing Your Energies

Daily Practices for Energy Balance

Each day presents a fresh opportunity to cultivate a balance between our feminine and masculine energies. A morning ritual can set the tone for the day, allowing you to consciously choose which energy you wish to lead with. For instance, you could start the day with a nurturing self-care routine such as self-touch or dancing to tap into your feminine energy, or an invigorating workout to ignite your masculine energy.

Throughout the day, pay attention to your energy levels and emotions. When you feel drained or overwhelmed, it could be a sign that your energies are out of balance. Take a few moments to pause and tune in to your body. What does it need? It could be a moment of quiet reflection, a nourishing meal, or a brisk walk outdoors.

Before retiring to bed, reflect on your day. Did you find a balance between doing and being, giving and receiving, asserting and yielding? If not, what can you do differently tomorrow? A nightly reflection can offer valuable insights into your energy patterns and guide your efforts toward energy balance.

Energy Healing Techniques

Energy healing techniques can be instrumental in balancing your feminine and masculine energies. These techniques work on the premise that our physical, emotional, and mental well-being is influenced by our energy flow. By balancing our energy flow, we can enhance our well-being and bring our feminine and masculine energies into harmony.

One such technique is Reiki, a Japanese method of energy healing. Reiki involves placing hands on or just above the body to channel healing energy and restore balance. It can be particularly effective in releasing energy blocks and promoting relaxation and well-being.

Another energy healing technique is Qigong, an ancient Chinese practice that combines movement, meditation, and breath control. Regular practice of Qigong can help balance yin (feminine) and yang (masculine) energies, promoting physical, emotional, and mental balance.

It's important to note that while energy healing techniques can support your energy balance, they should be used as a complement to, not a substitute for, medical care.

Yoga and Meditation for Energy Balance

Yoga and meditation are powerful tools for harmonizing your feminine and masculine energies. These ancient practices promote mindfulness, inner peace, and balance.

In yoga, certain poses can stimulate either feminine or masculine energy. For instance, forward bends and restorative poses can help you tap into your feminine energy, promoting relaxation and introspection. On the other hand, standing poses and inversions can ignite your masculine energy, fostering strength and confidence.

Yoga also works with the concept of Ida and Pingala, the two main energy channels in the body representing feminine and masculine energies. By practicing specific sequences and breathing techniques, you can balance these energy channels and harmonize your feminine and masculine energies.

Meditation, on the other hand, allows you to observe your thoughts and emotions without judgment, fostering self-awareness and inner peace. With regular practice, you can cultivate a balanced state of mind, where feminine qualities of intuition and empathy coexist with masculine qualities of logic and focus.

Through these practices, you can explore the dance of energies within you, experiencing the fluid interplay of the feminine and masculine, the harmonious blend of yin and yang. You can learn to honor and express both energies, fostering a sense of balance, wholeness, and authenticity.

So, engage with these practices, explore their depth, and experience their transformative power. Let them guide you towards inner balance, towards a harmonious dance of energies, towards a deeper connection with your true self.

Celebrating the Divine Union

Understanding the Divine Union

Picture the sky at dawn, a canvas painted with hues of orange and blue, neither fully day nor completely night. This moment of transition, when day and night merge into one, symbolizes the Divine Union - the harmonious convergence of feminine and masculine energies. A state where both energies are not only balanced but are also working together in a beautiful, seamless synergy.

This Divine Union is not an end state but a dynamic equilibrium, an ever-evolving dance where both energies are given the space to express and integrate. It's a state of wholeness, where we honor and embody both our nurturing, intuitive feminine energy and our assertive, logical masculine energy.

Rituals for Celebrating the Divine Union

Celebrating the Divine Union can be a potent way to acknowledge and honor the balance of energies within us. Rituals, with their symbolic actions and focused intentions, can serve as anchors, helping us connect more deeply with this state of inner unity.

One such ritual could be a simple candle ceremony. Light two candles representing the feminine and masculine energies. Meditate on the unique qualities of each as you light them. Then, slowly bring the two candles together, letting their flames merge into one, symbolizing the Divine Union. As you perform this ritual, set an intention to honor and balance both energies within you.

Another ritual could involve journaling. Write down the qualities of your feminine and masculine energies and how they manifest in your life. Reflect on how these two energies interact and balance each other. Express your gratitude for the wisdom and capabilities each energy brings to your life.

The Divine Union in Relationships and Personal Growth

The celebration of the Divine Union extends beyond our inner world; it also influences our relationships and personal development. In our relationships, the Divine Union manifests as a balance of giving and receiving, expressing and listening, leading and supporting. It allows us to build connections that are based on mutual respect, understanding, and equality.

In terms of personal growth, the Divine Union propels us to become more integrated and balanced individuals. It encourages us to be receptive and intuitive, yet also assertive and logical. It guides us to be nurturing and empathetic, yet also independent and confident. This balance fosters holistic personal growth, enabling us to navigate life with a richer array of skills and perspectives.

Celebrating the Divine Union is a beautiful testament to our wholeness. It's an acknowledgment of our multifaceted nature and a commitment to harmonizing our diverse energies. By honoring the Divine Union, we honor ourselves, our wholeness, our divinity. In this dance of energies, each step, each sway, each turn brings us closer to our authentic self, the self that embodies and embraces the Divine Feminine and the inner masculine in a harmonious union. So, let's continue to dance, to celebrate, and to honor this beautiful union within us.

As we move forward from this chapter, we carry with us the understanding of our diverse energies, some techniques to harmonize them, and the celebration of their divine union. In the chapters ahead, we will explore how this understanding and harmony translate into various aspects of our daily lives. From self-care to relationships to emotional healing, the dance of the Divine Feminine and inner masculine influences every part of our existence, guiding us toward a more balanced, authentic, and fulfilling life. So, dear reader, let's turn the page and continue our exploration.

Chapter Five

The Sacred Art of Self-Care

Tending to ourselves is similar to tending to a garden. In life, we often find ourselves playing multiple roles. We are daughters, mothers, partners, friends, and professionals. In the midst of juggling these roles and responsibilities, we sometimes forget the most important role – being our own caretaker. Just as a gardener tends to each plant with love and dedication, we need to tend to our own needs, to nurture our body, mind, and soul. This chapter is dedicated to self-care, an essential practice that forms the bedrock of the divine feminine journey.

Prioritizing Your Well-being

Recognizing Signs of Burnout

Burnout is a state of chronic physical and emotional exhaustion, often accompanied by feelings of cynicism and detachment. It's like running a marathon with no finish line in sight, each step draining your energy until all that's left is a profound sense of fatigue and disillusionment.

Recognizing the signs of burnout is the first step towards prioritizing your well-being. These signs can manifest physically as frequent headaches, sleep disturbances, or a weakened immune system. Emotionally, you might feel a sense of apathy, irritability, or hopelessness. You might also notice changes in your behavior such as procrastination, withdrawal from social activities, or reliance on substances like caffeine or alcohol to get through the day.

If you find yourself experiencing these symptoms, it's a clear signal that your well-being needs immediate attention. Remember, you can't pour from an empty cup. You need to replenish your reserves before you can take care of others or meet your responsibilities effectively.

Creating a Personalized Self-Care Plan

A self-care plan is a proactive strategy to maintain and enhance your well-being. It's like a roadmap, guiding you towards activities and practices that nourish you on all levels – physical, mental, emotional, and spiritual.

Begin by identifying activities that make you feel good. It could be a brisk walk in the park, a relaxing bath, a yoga session, or a quiet time with a book. Next, consider your emotional and mental well-being. This could involve journaling, meditation, therapy, or simply spending time with loved ones.

Remember, your self-care plan should be flexible, reflecting your unique needs and circumstances. It's not about adhering to a rigid schedule or an unrealistic routine. It's about listening to your body, honoring your feelings, and giving yourself permission to take care of your well-being.

The Role of Mindfulness in Self-Care

Mindfulness – the practice of being fully present and engaged in the current moment – plays a crucial role in self-care. It's a spotlight, illuminating your needs, feelings, and responses, enabling you to take care of your well-being more effectively.

Mindfulness can help you tune into your body's signals, alerting you to physical stress or fatigue. It can help you recognize your emotional state, allowing you to address feelings of anxiety, sadness, or frustration. It can also help you identify negative thought patterns, allowing you to challenge and change them.

You can practice mindfulness in various ways – through meditation, mindful eating, mindful walking, mindful self-touch, or simply pausing for a few moments to take a few deep breaths. Whichever method you choose, the key is to bring your full attention to the present moment, observing your experiences without judgment or distraction.

In the words of Thich Nhat Hanh, a renowned mindfulness teacher,

> "The present moment is filled with joy and happiness. If you are attentive, you will see it."

Let this be your guiding principle as you prioritize your well-being and embark on your self-care journey. It's a gentle reminder that every moment holds an opportunity for self-care, for self-love, and for self-nurturing. So, be attentive, be mindful, be present – and watch as you cultivate a deep sense of well-being and balance.

Rituals for Self-Care

Morning and Evening Rituals

The sun's first rays break the night's darkness, the gentle hush as the world stirs awake - there's something inherently magical about mornings. This magic lays the perfect foundation for a morning self-care ritual. As the day dawns, take a few moments to connect with yourself. You could start with a gentle stretch to awaken your body, followed by a few minutes of imagining intentionally how you would like to feel and a few things you want to happen that day. This can help set the tone for the entire day.

Hydrate with a glass of warm water with a dash of lemon, a gentle detox, and a refreshing start to the day. Follow this with a nourishing breakfast, mindfully enjoying each bite. This isn't just about feeding your body; it's about nourishing your soul.

As the day unfolds, stay tuned to your needs. Take short breaks to stretch, hydrate, or simply breathe. Remember, self-care isn't a chore to be squeezed into your day; it's a lifestyle that intertwines with your daily routine.

As daylight fades into the soft hues of dusk, it's time to unwind with an evening ritual. This could be as simple as a warm bath infused with essential oils, a calming yoga sequence, some deep breathing, or writing in your gratitude journal.

Before surrendering to sleep, take a few moments to release the day's stress and worries. Visualize them flowing out of you with each exhale, leaving you lighter and more relaxed. If something challenging happens in the day, revise it. How can you retell the story or rewrite it so that you can let it go before falling asleep? This practice of conscious release and revision aids restful sleep, a crucial part of self-care.

Full Moon and New Moon Rituals

The moon, with its rhythmic waxing and waning, has been a source of fascination and a symbol of the feminine since ancient times. Aligning your self-care rituals with the lunar cycles can be a powerful way to connect with nature's rhythms and your feminine energy.

The full moon, with its radiant glow, symbolizes completion and celebration. Create a full moon ritual that focuses on gratitude and release. Start by lighting a candle, symbolizing the full moon's light. Reflect on the past lunar cycle, acknowledging your achievements and expressing gratitude. Then, write down what you wish to release or let go of, and safely burn the paper, symbolizing release.

The new moon, on the other hand, marks a time of beginnings. It's a blank canvas, inviting you to set intentions for the lunar cycle ahead. For your new moon ritual, sit comfortably, perhaps with a clear quartz crystal to amplify your intentions. Reflect on your desires and goals for the coming weeks, and write them down in a journal. As you do this, visualize your intentions coming to fruition, and trust in the universe to guide you.

Creating Your Own Personal Rituals

Make self-care personal to you. Don't hesitate to create your own personal rituals that resonate with your individual needs and preferences. Your ritual could involve dancing to your favorite music, painting, soaking in a bubble bath, or simply sitting in silence. The key is to choose activities that you enjoy and that make you feel nurtured and centered.

When creating your rituals, consider incorporating elements that engage all your senses. This could include burning incense for a calming scent, playing soothing music for aural pleasure, sipping herbal tea for taste, using a soft blanket for touch, and placing flowers or crystals for visual appeal.

Remember, your self-care rituals don't need to be elaborate or time-consuming. They just need to be meaningful to you. Whether it's a five-minute meditation or an hour-long yoga session, what matters is that it helps you connect with yourself, soothe your soul, and honor your divine feminine energy.

As you weave these rituals into your daily life, they become gentle reminders to pause, to connect, and to care for yourself. They become sacred spaces in your day, sanctuaries where you can retreat from the world and commune with your inner self. They become the threads that weave self-care into the tapestry of your life, coloring it with hues of self-love, self-respect, and self-nurturing. And in this colorful tapestry, you'll find a reflection of your divine feminine energy, vibrant and radiant, and blooming.

The Importance of Rest and Rejuvenation

A garden, after a season of growth, lies fallow under the winter snow, replenishing its nutrients for the coming spring. The moon, after reaching its fullness, retreats into darkness, only to emerge renewed in the next lunar cycle. Similarly, our bodies and minds, after periods of activity, require rest and rejuvenation to maintain balance and vitality.

Understanding Your Body's Natural Rhythms

Our bodies operate on a 24-hour cycle known as the circadian rhythm. This internal clock, influenced by light and darkness, governs various physiological processes such as sleep, digestion, and hormone production. Aligning our self-care practices with our body's natural rhythms can enhance our well-being and energy levels.

During the day, as sunlight prompts our bodies to awake and be active, it's beneficial to engage in stimulating activities such as work, exercise, and social interactions. As evening falls and darkness sets in, our bodies naturally shift into a state of rest and repair. This is an ideal time to engage in calming activities such as reading, meditation, or gentle stretching.

By understanding and aligning with our body's natural rhythms, we can optimize our energy levels, enhance our productivity, and promote restful sleep. It's like flowing with the current of a river, moving smoothly and effortlessly, rather than against it, struggling and straining.

The Science of Sleep

Sleep is not merely a passive state of unconsciousness but a vital process of restoration and rejuvenation. During sleep, our bodies repair tissues, produce hormones and consolidate memories. Our brains, too, are busy during sleep, clearing out toxins and processing information from the day.

Research has shown that consistent, quality sleep is linked to numerous health benefits, including enhanced immune function, improved mental health, and reduced risk of chronic diseases. On the flip side, sleep deprivation can lead to a host of health issues, including fatigue, impaired cognition, mood swings, and weakened immunity.

Creating a sleep-friendly environment can significantly improve the quality of your sleep. This might include keeping your bedroom dark, quiet, and cool, investing in a comfortable mattress and pillows, and establishing a regular sleep schedule. Limiting exposure to screens before bed and avoiding caffeine and alcohol in the evening can also promote restful sleep.

Techniques for Deep Relaxation

Deep relaxation is a state of profound physical and mental calm that can be achieved through various techniques. Unlike the passive relaxation we experience while lounging on a couch or watching TV, deep relaxation involves actively guiding the body and mind into a state of calm and ease.

One of the most effective techniques for deep relaxation is progressive muscle relaxation. This involves tensing and then relaxing each muscle group, starting from your toes and working your way up to your head. As you release the tension from your muscles, you'll likely find that your mind, too, becomes calmer and quieter.

Another powerful relaxation technique is deep breathing. By slowing and deepening your breath, you can activate your body's relaxation response, reducing stress and promoting a sense of calm. Try inhaling deeply through your nose, holding your breath for a few seconds, and then exhaling slowly through your mouth. Repeat this for a few minutes, focusing your attention on the sensation of your breath flowing in and out.

Using imagination intentionally is yet another technique for deep relaxation. Close your eyes and imagine a scene that implies your desire is fulfilled. Maybe it's a place, such as a beach, a forest, or a garden. Perhaps it is a conversation with a loved one hearing them say something to you that makes you feel good or congratulating you on an achievement. Engage all your senses in this scene. What do you see, hear, smell, feel, taste? By immersing yourself in this imaginal scene, you can induce a state of deep relaxation, tranquility, and good feelings.

Exploring self-touch purely for the pleasure and experience can be a deeply enriching and empowering practice. It allows you to connect with your body on a profound level, fostering self-awareness and understanding. It's about honoring your sensations and desires in the present moment, rather than focusing solely on achieving a specific outcome. Self-touch is not exclusively sexual. It can encompass a wide range of sensations and experiences beyond just arousal. Engaging in gentle self-touch, such as massage or simply exploring different textures on your skin, can be incredibly soothing and nurturing. It's about nurturing a positive relationship with your body and acknowledging the vast spectrum of sensations it can offer beyond purely sexual ones. If you are interested in being guided through a self-touch practice, get my free 3-day video series on pelvic freedom which is found in the Resources section. Self-touch is a special practice personally and one that I facilitate and encourage for my clients.

By incorporating rest, sleep, and deep relaxation into our self-care routine, we provide our bodies and minds with the downtime they need to replenish and rejuvenate. It's an act of kindness and respect towards ourselves, an acknowledgment of our inherent worth and dignity. It's a recognition that we, too, like the garden and the moon, need periods of rest and renewal to maintain our balance and vitality. So, let's honor our need for rest. Let's embrace the sweet surrender of sleep. Let's indulge in the bliss of deep relaxation.

Nourishing Your Body, Mind and Soul

Nutritional Choices for Optimal Health

Just as a gardener meticulously selects the best nutrients to enrich the soil for her plants, it's vital for us to choose nutritious foods that nourish our bodies. Our dietary choices have a profound impact on our physical health, mood, and energy levels.

Consider adopting a balanced diet filled with a variety of whole foods. Incorporate plenty of fresh fruits and vegetables, which are packed with essential vitamins, minerals, and antioxidants. Opt for whole grains over refined ones to benefit from their fiber content and nutrient density.

Lean proteins, such as beans, lentils, eggs, and lean meats, are essential for building and repairing tissues. Healthy fats, found in foods like avocados, nuts, seeds, and olive oil, support hormonal balance and brain function.

For optimal health, cutting out certain foods, including sugar, alcohol, and processed foods, can be beneficial. Here are some specifics:

Added Sugars: Sugary foods and beverages contribute to weight gain, and dental issues, and can increase the risk of chronic diseases like type 2 diabetes and heart disease.

Alcohol: While occasional alcohol consumption may have some health benefits, excessive drinking can lead to liver disease, increased risk of certain cancers, mental health issues, and addiction.

Processed Foods: Processed foods often contain high amounts of unhealthy fats, sodium, and artificial additives. These foods lack essential nutrients and can contribute to weight gain, inflammation, and an increased risk of chronic diseases.

Refined Grains: Refined grains like white bread, white rice, and pasta made from white flour have been stripped of their nutrients and fiber during processing. They can cause rapid spikes in blood sugar levels and contribute to weight gain and insulin resistance.

Trans Fats: Trans fats are artificial fats found in partially hydrogenated oils, often used in processed and fried foods to improve shelf life and texture. They raise bad cholesterol levels (LDL) and lower good cholesterol levels (HDL), increasing the risk of heart disease.

By cutting out these unhealthy foods and focusing on a diet rich in whole, nutrient-dense foods like fruits, vegetables, lean proteins, whole grains, and healthy fats, you can optimize your health and well-being. Additionally, consulting with a healthcare provider or registered dietitian can provide personalized guidance and support on making dietary changes.

Remember, your body is your temple, the sacred vessel that houses your divine feminine energy. Honor it by making nutritional choices that support optimal health and vitality.

Mental Stimulation and Lifelong Learning

Our minds, like muscles, need consistent stimulation to stay sharp and agile. Engaging in lifelong learning and mental stimulation is a potent way to nourish your mind and maintain cognitive health.

Keep your mind active and engaged by reading, solving puzzles, or learning a new skill. Stimulate your creativity by painting, writing, or playing a musical instrument. There's a world of knowledge out there waiting to be explored. Whether you're interested in art, science, history, or philosophy, dive in and let your mind soak in the wisdom.

Beyond merely acquiring knowledge, strive to understand, question, and reflect on what you learn. This not only enhances your cognitive skills but also fosters personal growth and self-awareness.

Spiritual Practices for Soul Nourishment

Just as we nourish our bodies with nutritious foods and our minds with stimulating activities, our souls, too, need nourishment. Spiritual practices can provide this nourishment, helping us connect with our inner selves and the world around us on a deeper level.

Meditation is a powerful spiritual practice that fosters mindfulness, inner peace, and self-awareness. It allows us to connect with our inner selves, to tap into our intuition, and to cultivate a deep sense of inner peace. Remember that walking, movement, and dance can become a meditation. It does not always have to be sitting in a traditional meditation posture.

Prayer or chanting, regardless of religious affiliation, can also be a potent source of solace and strength. They provide a channel for expressing our hopes, fears, gratitude, and aspirations, fostering a sense of connection with the divine.

Spending time in nature, too, can be a deeply spiritual experience. It allows us to feel connected to the universe, to appreciate the beauty and wonder of creation, and to feel a sense of awe and reverence for life itself.

Remember, nourishing your soul is as important as nourishing your body and mind. So, make time for spiritual practices that resonate with you, that bring you joy and peace, that help you connect with your true self.

As we close this chapter, let's carry forth the understanding that self-care is not a luxury or an afterthought. It's a fundamental aspect of our journey towards embracing the divine feminine. It's about honoring our needs, nourishing our bodies, minds, and souls, and cultivating a deep sense of self-love and self-respect. As we turn our attention towards these practices, we create a nurturing environment for our divine feminine energy to thrive and flourish.

Let's continue to explore this path together, embracing the wisdom, the love, and the transformative power of the divine feminine. As we move into the next chapter, we'll delve into how this energy shapes our relationships, bringing depth, connection, and balance into our interactions with others.

Chapter Six

The Divine Feminine: Shaping Relationships with Authenticity and Empathy

Waves serve as nature's poignant illustration of the perpetual ebb and flow of life, mirroring the rhythmic cycles of growth, change, and renewal that characterize our existence. As we watch the rhythmic dance of the waves, they ebb and flow, each movement distinct yet part of a harmonious whole - a captivating dance of give and take. Our relationships, much like these waves, are a delicate balance of giving and receiving, expressing and understanding, leading and following. In this chapter, we will explore how the Divine Feminine can shape our relationships, guiding us toward deeper connections, mutual understanding, and authentic expression.

Shaping Relationships with Feminine Energy

With the Divine Feminine as our compass, we can navigate the waters of our relationships with greater awareness and intention. Whether it's a friendship, a romantic relationship, or a professional connection, the Divine Feminine can guide us to create harmonious and fulfilling relationships.

Attracting Harmonious Relationships

In our quest for harmonious relationships, it's essential to remember that like attracts like. The energy we emit is the energy we attract. When we embody the Divine Feminine, radiating love, compassion, and authenticity, we naturally attract relationships that mirror these qualities.

So, how do we attract harmonious relationships? The first step is and truly ALWAYS is to cultivate these qualities within ourselves. Practice self-love and self-compassion, honor your authenticity, and nurture your emotional well-being. This isn't a one-time task, but an ongoing practice, a commitment to your personal growth and happiness. Remember it is always about YOU. Choose yourself every day and make yourself a priority.

Next, imagine the kind of relationships you wish to attract. How do you want to *feel* in these relationships? What values do you want these relationships to reflect? Who are you being in this moment to feel this as true **now**?

Your state guides everything – your thoughts and feelings come from your state. Who do you want to be in your ideal relationship? For example, if you're single and you desire a long-term relationship, can you play with the identity of a *happy, loving wife*? It might feel foreign. I know it does for me, but I continue to play in this state and explore it. How does this identity of a *happy, loving wife* guide your actions? On a personal note, I discovered I hadn't allowed myself to feel like I was deserving to be a happy, loving wife. Somewhere along the way, I let my masculine take over. I had to be an independent, strong, single mom and do it all on my own. It's been in the recent past, that my mentor introduced this ideal state of *Happy, Loving Wife*. When I remember to play in this state and let it lead, I let myself embody it. It could be simply feeling the wedding ring on your finger or feeling a vague sense of relief right now because you already have the loving relationship you most desire. Embodying the happy, loving state can then guide your interactions with your significant other and avoid potential arguments. Often when we are choosing to feel happy and loving in most situations, it instantly drops the need to argue or be right.

Hold this identity in your heart, explore new identities, and let it move your actions and choices.

Healing Relationship Patterns

We all carry patterns in our relationships, some beneficial, others not so much. These patterns often stem from our past experiences and subconscious beliefs, shaping our interactions and relationships in profound ways.

Identifying and healing these patterns is a key aspect of shaping relationships with the Divine Feminine. This involves reflecting on your past and present relationships and noticing any recurring themes or patterns. Do you often feel unheard or undervalued? Do you tend to attract emotionally unavailable partners? Do you often put others' needs before your own?

I've been able to identify my pattern of overgiving to receive love or my perception of receiving love. I have chosen partners who are emotionally unavailable and not able to reciprocate fully. Then resentment builds for overgiving and underreceiving. Recognizing patterns in our thoughts, behaviors, and emotions allows us to understand ourselves better and make positive changes. It gives us the ability to break free from harmful cycles and cultivate healthier habits. Plus, it can lead to greater self-compassion and acceptance, which are essential components of healing and personal growth.

Once you've identified these patterns, explore their roots. Was there an event in your past that led to this pattern? Is there a belief or fear fueling this pattern? This exploration can be challenging, bringing up painful memories or uncomfortable emotions, but it's a crucial step toward healing and transformation.

To heal these patterns, you might need to challenge your beliefs, heal your emotional wounds, or change your behavior. This is not an easy task, and it's okay to seek support. A therapist or a support group can provide guidance and encouragement on this healing journey.

The Power of Vulnerability in Relationships

Vulnerability is often seen as a weakness, a flaw to be hidden away. But in reality, vulnerability is a strength, a gateway to deeper connections and authentic relationships.

Being vulnerable in a relationship means expressing your feelings openly and honestly, even when it's uncomfortable. It means admitting your mistakes, asking for help when you need it, and showing up as your true self.

Embracing vulnerability can be scary, as it involves exposing our insecurities and fears. But it's in this raw, unfiltered expression of ourselves that true connections are formed. When we show up in our vulnerability, we permit others to do the same, creating a space for authenticity and mutual understanding.

Practicing vulnerability in a relationship could mean sharing your fears and insecurities with your partner, expressing your needs and desires, or opening up about your past. Remember, vulnerability is not about oversharing or being emotionally needy. It's about sharing your inner world with someone you trust, in a way that fosters connection and intimacy.

In conclusion, shaping relationships with feminine energy involves attracting harmonious relationships, healing relationship patterns, and embracing vulnerability. It's about creating relationships that not only fulfill our needs and desires but also reflect our values and authenticity. By embodying the Divine Feminine in our relationships, we can cultivate deeper connections, mutual understanding, and a profound sense of belonging and love.

The Role of Intuition in Building Relationships

Developing Your Intuitive Abilities

Intuition, that subtle inner voice that gently nudges us in a particular direction, is a powerful asset in the realm of relationships. Often, our intuition can perceive the nuances of interactions and emotions that our conscious mind may overlook. To harness this innate wisdom, we must first cultivate our intuitive abilities.

One way to enhance your intuition is through regular meditation. By quieting the mind, we create a space for our intuition to surface. Close your eyes, take a few deep breaths, and focus your attention inward. You can focus your attention on the brow point, the spot between your eyebrows, and a bit above. Yogically, this is referred to as the *third eye*. This area is physically where the pituitary gland is which regulates hormones such as serotonin – the feel-good hormone. It is also the home of intuition. When you focus on this area, it naturally stimulates serotonin and intuition development. Let go of any thoughts or distractions and simply observe the sensations, images, or feelings that arise. With practice, you will start recognizing these subtle whispers of your intuition.

Another effective way to develop your intuitive abilities is through mindfulness. By being fully present in each moment, we can tune into our gut feelings and hunches. Pay attention to your body's signals. You might feel a knot in your stomach, a flutter in your heart, or a chill down your spine. These sensations are often indicators of your intuitive responses.

In my journey of developing intuition, I've found that a significant portion of my work revolves around somatics - the deep exploration of the body's wisdom. Through somatic practices, I've come to understand that intuition isn't just a mental process; it's also deeply felt through the sensations and feelings within our bodies.

When we tune into these subtle bodily cues, we open ourselves up to a whole new realm of awareness. It's as if our bodies are speaking to us in their own language, offering insights and guidance that our rational minds may overlook. This is the essence of somatic intuition - the ability to listen to the whispers of our bodies and trust in their innate wisdom.

Developing this kind of body awareness is a transformative journey. It involves tuning into the nuances of our physical sensations, from the tingling of excitement to the tightening of fear. With practice, we can learn to decipher these signals and understand what they may be connected to - whether it's a hidden emotion, an unspoken truth, or a deeper knowing that transcends logic.

I share a practical exercise called "The Embodiment of Boundaries" from my somatic training and certification. It was profoundly impactful for me to gain insight and help me tap into my somatic intuition. As my gift to you, get the video here or find it in the Resources section. By integrating somatic practices into your daily life, you can cultivate a deeper connection with yourself and the world around you. Trust in the wisdom of your body, and let it guide you on your journey of intuition and self-discovery.

Trusting Your Gut Feelings

Once you've cultivated your intuitive abilities, the next step is to trust your gut feelings. Often, our intuition communicates through gut feelings or hunches. These feelings can provide valuable insights into our relationships, guiding us toward what feels right and warning us about potential red flags.

However, trusting your gut feelings can be challenging, especially when they contradict logical reasoning or external opinions. It requires courage to listen to your inner voice and to honor its wisdom.

One way to build trust in your gut feelings is to start small. Use your intuition to make minor decisions, like what to wear or what to eat. Notice how often your gut feelings lead you in the right direction. Gradually, as your confidence grows, you can rely on your intuition for more significant decisions, including those related to your relationships.

Using Intuition as a Guide in Relationships

In the context of relationships, intuition serves as an inner compass, guiding us towards healthy and fulfilling connections. It can help us discern the intentions of others, sense the underlying dynamics of interactions, and make decisions that align with our emotional well-being.

When entering a new relationship, your intuition can provide valuable insights. It can pick up on subtle cues about the person's character, helping you discern if they're trustworthy, respectful, and compatible with you. If something feels off, even if you can't pinpoint why, it's essential to heed your intuition. It's okay to take a step back, create some space, or even exit the relationship if it doesn't feel right.

In existing relationships, your intuition can help maintain harmony and understanding. It can guide you to express your feelings at the right time, to offer support when your partner needs it, or to establish boundaries when necessary. By using your intuition as a guide, you can navigate your relationships with greater awareness, authenticity, and empathy.

The dance of relationships, much like the dance of the waves, is a delicate balance of giving and receiving, expressing and understanding, leading and following. By embracing our intuition, we can navigate this dance with grace and wisdom. We become more attuned to our needs and emotions, more responsive to our partners, and more authentic in our interactions. So, as we continue to explore the divine feminine in relationships, let's remember to honor our intuition, trust its wisdom, and let it guide us toward connections that nourish our souls and enrich our lives.

Cultivating Empathy and Compassion

Understanding the Difference Between Empathy and Sympathy

Picture a friend sharing a personal struggle with you. Your heart aches as you listen to their story. Two potential responses arise within you: empathy, where you vicariously experience your friend's feelings, and sympathy, where you acknowledge their distress but remain emotionally detached.

Empathy, a cornerstone of the Divine Feminine, involves immersing yourself in the emotional world of another, feeling their joy, their pain, their hopes, and their fears as if they were your own. It's a shared experience, bridging the gap between self and other.

Sympathy, on the other hand, is a recognition of another's distress coupled with a desire to comfort, but it lacks the shared emotional experience that characterizes empathy. It's like standing on the shore, watching someone struggle in the water, while empathy is diving in to be with them.

While both responses have their place, empathy holds transformative potential. It fosters deep connections, facilitates emotional healing, and cultivates compassion, making it an invaluable tool in building authentic, nurturing relationships.

Practicing Compassionate Listening

Active, attentive listening is an act of love, a form of generosity, a manifestation of the Divine Feminine in action. And when underpinned by empathy, it transforms into compassionate listening, a practice that goes beyond merely hearing words.

Compassionate listening invites us to tune into the emotional undertones of a conversation, to be present with the speaker's feelings, and to offer our undivided attention and empathy. It's not about problem-solving or offering advice, but about providing a safe, empathic space where feelings can be expressed and validated.

To practice compassionate listening, start by creating a quiet, undisturbed space for conversation. Ground yourself in the present moment, setting aside your judgments and preconceptions. As the other person shares, tune into their words, their tone, their body language. What are their words communicating? What emotions are surfacing?

Respond with empathy and validation, acknowledging their feelings without trying to change or fix them. Phrases like "That sounds really tough," or "I can see why you're upset," can affirm their feelings and convey your empathic understanding. Remember, compassionate listening is about being present and empathic, allowing the other person to feel seen, heard, and understood.

Empathy as a Tool for Conflict Resolution

In the landscape of relationships, conflicts are like rocky terrains that can either trip us up or prompt us to find new paths. Navigating these terrains calls for empathy, a vital tool that can transform conflicts into opportunities for growth and deeper understanding.

When conflicts arise, our instinct may be to defend our position, to prove our point, to win the argument. But what if, instead, we chose to empathize? What if we tried to see the situation from the other person's perspective, to understand their feelings, to validate their experience?

Empathy encourages us to step out of our defensive stance and step into the shoes of the other person. It invites us to see the situation through their eyes, to feel their emotions, to understand their perspective. This shift in perspective can diffuse tension, foster understanding, and pave the way for constructive dialogue.

Furthermore, expressing our feelings and needs in an empathic manner can facilitate resolution. This involves speaking from the heart, expressing how we feel, and what we need, without blaming or criticizing. Phrases like "I feel upset when... I need..." can communicate our feelings and needs clearly and empathically.

Cultivating empathy and compassion is a transformative practice that can enrich our relationships. It invites deeper connections, fosters mutual understanding, and facilitates conflict resolution. As we embrace this practice, we create relationships that reflect the nurturing, empathic, and loving essence of the Divine Feminine.

Setting Boundaries: The Act of Self-Love

An example of a boundary you might set with a friend or lover could be regarding personal space and time. For instance, if you have a friend who often drops by unannounced and expects you to drop everything to spend time with them, you might set a boundary by explaining that while you value their friendship, you need advance notice before visits and you also need some alone time to recharge. This communicates your needs clearly and helps establish a healthy balance in the relationship. Boundaries constitute a crucial aspect of self-care and self-love, reflecting our respect for our needs, feelings, and values. In this section, we will discuss how to identify, communicate, and enforce your personal boundaries.

Identifying Your Personal Boundaries

Recognizing our personal boundaries is the first step towards asserting them. Our boundaries reflect our unique needs, values, and experiences, and hence, they vary from person to person. For some, a boundary could be needing solitude after a long day at work. For others, it might be preferring texts over phone calls, or not discussing certain topics.

To identify your boundaries, tune into your feelings and intuition. Pay attention to situations that leave you feeling drained, uncomfortable, or resentful. These feelings are often signals that your boundaries have been crossed. Reflect on your values, your needs, and your past experiences. What matters most to you in your interactions with others? What makes you feel respected and valued? Your answers to these questions can provide valuable insights into your personal boundaries.

Communicating Your Boundaries Effectively

Once you have identified your boundaries, the next step is to communicate them effectively. This involves expressing your boundaries clearly, confidently, and respectfully. It's not about being defensive or confrontational, but about asserting your needs in a positive and assertive manner.

When communicating your boundaries, use "I" statements to express your feelings and needs. For example, instead of saying, "You always call me late at night," you could say, "I need to have quiet time in the evenings. Could we please schedule our calls earlier?" This way, you express your boundaries without blaming or criticizing the other person.

Remember, it's okay to say no when a request or a situation conflicts with your boundaries. Saying no is not a rejection of the person, but an affirmation of your needs and limits. It's a sign of self-respect and self-care, and it communicates to others that you value your well-being.

Dealing with Boundary Violations

Despite our best efforts to communicate our boundaries, there might be instances when they're violated. This could be due to a misunderstanding, a difference in expectations, or a disregard for our boundaries.

When a boundary violation occurs, it's important to address it promptly and assertively. Express your feelings, clarify your boundaries, and communicate your expectations for future interactions. For instance, you could say, "I felt uncomfortable when you shared my news with others. I value my privacy, and I'd appreciate it if you could check with me before sharing my personal information."

In some cases, you might need to enforce consequences for repeated boundary violations. This could involve distancing yourself from the person or seeking support from a mediator or a counselor. It's crucial to remember that you have the right to protect your boundaries and to take steps to ensure they're respected.

Cultivating and asserting personal boundaries is an ongoing process. It involves self-awareness, assertiveness, and resilience. It's not always easy, and it can sometimes feel uncomfortable. But it's a crucial aspect of self-care and self-love, reflecting our respect for our own needs, feelings, and values. By setting and maintaining our boundaries, we not only protect our well-being but also enhance the quality of our relationships. We create a space where authenticity, respect, and empathy can flourish, mirroring the nurturing and empowering essence of the Divine Feminine.

As we move forward, let's remember to honor our personal boundaries, to assert them with confidence and grace, and to protect them with resolve and strength. In this way, we not only cultivate self-love and self-respect, but also foster authentic, respectful, and fulfilling relationships. In the upcoming chapters, we will further explore the myriad ways in which the Divine Feminine can guide us on our path of personal growth and transformation.

Chapter Seven

Divine Feminine: Healing Emotional Wounds and Cultivating Resilience

Consider an exquisite porcelain vase knocked off its pedestal. It shatters into myriad pieces, the fragments scattered across the floor. But then, through a process known as kintsugi, a Japanese art form, gold-dusted lacquer is meticulously applied to bind the fragments together. The vase, once broken, now stands whole again, its fractures highlighted rather than hidden, making it even more beautiful. This concept of finding beauty in the broken is a fitting analogy for our exploration into the realm of emotional wounds, their impact, and the healing process.

Just as the golden seams in the repaired vase tell a tale of resilience, so do our emotional wounds. They are the remnants of past traumas, experiences that have shaped us, for better or worse. They are the echoes of our childhood, the residues of our relationships, the scars of our struggles. But they are not just symbols of pain; they are also signposts for healing, growth, and transformation. Let's explore this further.

Understanding Emotional Wounds

Recognizing the Impact of Childhood Trauma

Childhood, the formative phase of our lives, lays the groundwork for our future selves. Positive experiences during this time can foster self-esteem, resilience, and healthy relationships. However, adverse experiences, such as neglect, abuse, or witnessing violence, can leave deep emotional wounds. These childhood traumas can significantly impact mental health and well-being, often extending into adulthood.

Childhood trauma can affect our ability to trust others, form healthy relationships, and regulate emotions. It may lead to patterns of self-destructive behavior, difficulties with intimacy, or an overriding sense of fear and insecurity. Acknowledging the impact of these early traumas is a crucial step in the healing process. It's about understanding that our emotional wounds are not signs of weakness but marks of survival.

The Connection Between Emotional Wounds and Physical Health

Our minds and bodies are intimately connected, constantly communicating and influencing each other. Thus, it's not surprising that our emotional health can have a significant impact on our physical health. It's like a ripple effect; emotional pain can trigger physical symptoms. This connection is especially evident when it comes to emotional wounds.

Unresolved emotional wounds can manifest as physical symptoms such as headaches, digestive issues, sleep disturbances, and even chronic pain. They can also contribute to the development of illnesses such as heart disease, diabetes, and other serious health conditions. The mind-body connection underscores the importance of addressing and healing emotional wounds, not just for our emotional well-being but for our physical health as well.

Emotional Wounds and Self-Sabotage

When we've been hurt in the past, we may unknowingly adopt behaviors that protect us from experiencing that pain again. These defense mechanisms may serve us in the short term, but over time, they can evolve into patterns of self-sabotage that hinder our growth and happiness.

For instance, if we've been rejected or abandoned in the past, we may avoid getting too close to people or rejecting them before they can reject us. If we've been criticized or belittled, we may hold back from expressing our thoughts or asserting our needs.

While these behaviors might give us a sense of safety, they can also keep us stuck in our pain, reinforcing our emotional wounds rather than healing them. Recognizing these patterns of self-sabotage is the first step towards breaking free from them and moving towards healing and growth.

Understanding emotional wounds involves recognizing the impact of childhood trauma, acknowledging the connection between emotional wounds and physical health, and identifying patterns of self-sabotage. It's about peeling back the layers of pain and defense mechanisms to reveal the raw, tender wounds beneath. It's about looking our wounds in the eye and saying, "I see you. I acknowledge you. I am ready to heal you." This readiness to face our wounds, to embrace our brokenness, is the first step towards healing. It's the golden lacquer that starts to bind our fragments together, leading us towards wholeness, resilience, and beauty, much like the exquisitely repaired vase.

So, as we dive deeper into the process of emotional healing, let's remember that our emotional wounds are not our final destination, but our starting point. They are the catalysts for our healing, the fuel for our transformation, the cracks that let the light in.

In the words of Leonard Cohen,

"There is a crack in everything. That's how the light gets in."

Let's let the light in and embark on the healing journey with courage, compassion, and the empowering wisdom of the Divine Feminine.

The Power of Forgiveness

The Process of Forgiveness

Imagine standing in front of a blank canvas, a paintbrush poised in your hand. This canvas represents the canvas of your emotions, waiting to be transformed. You dip your brush into a vibrant color, representing the hurt and resentment you've been carrying. With deliberate strokes, you begin to paint, expressing all the pain and anger onto the canvas.

As the colors blend and merge, they create a chaotic swirl of emotions, disrupting the stillness of the canvas. But with each brushstroke, you release a little bit of the hurt you've been holding onto. You paint until the canvas is filled with a raw and honest expression of your emotions.

And then, just as suddenly as you began, you take a step back and observe your creation. In that moment, you realize that by expressing your pain through art, you've allowed yourself to release it. The painting serves as a symbol of your forgiveness, a testament to your willingness to let go of old wounds and embrace healing.

Forgiveness is a process, often a complex and lengthy one. It begins with acknowledging the hurt and pain caused by another's actions or words and allowing ourselves to feel the associated emotions. This acknowledgment is not about dwelling on the hurt or reliving the pain, but about validating our feelings and experiences. It's about honoring our truth and standing up for our emotional well-being.

The next step in the process of forgiveness is making a conscious choice to let go of resentment and anger. This choice is not about excusing the person's actions or forgetting the hurt caused. It's about freeing ourselves from the heavy burden of resentment and opening our hearts to healing and peace. It's about making a conscious decision to let go of resentment and anger, even if the person who hurt us doesn't apologize or acknowledge their actions. It's about choosing love over fear, understanding over resentment, and healing over hurt.

Forgiving Yourself

While forgiving others can be challenging, forgiving ourselves is often even harder. We tend to be our harshest critics, holding onto guilt and regret long after the event has passed. Yet, self-forgiveness is a vital part of healing our emotional wounds.

Forgiving ourselves involves recognizing our mistakes, acknowledging the harm caused, and expressing genuine remorse. It requires us to challenge our self-critical inner voice.

But acknowledging our mistakes is not enough. We also need to extend compassion and understanding to ourselves. We need to remind ourselves that we are human, that we are fallible, and that it's okay to make mistakes. We need to remember that every mistake is an opportunity for growth, for learning, and for becoming a better version of ourselves.

Self-forgiveness is not about absolving ourselves of responsibility or ignoring the consequences of our actions. It's about acknowledging our mistakes, learning from them, and making amends where possible. It's about releasing guilt and regret, allowing us to move forward with wisdom and compassion. Self-forgiveness is not a one-time act, but a lifelong practice. It's a commitment to ourselves, a promise to treat ourselves with kindness and compassion, regardless of our past mistakes. It's a journey towards self-love and self-acceptance, where every step taken is a step towards healing and inner peace.

Forgiveness and Freedom

Forgiveness, whether towards ourselves or others, is a pathway to freedom. It liberates us from the prison of resentment and bitterness, allowing us to experience life in all its richness and beauty. It frees our hearts to love, our minds to explore, and our souls to soar. It brings light to our shadows, hope to our despair, and peace to our turmoil.

Forgiveness also frees us to live in the present, rather than being anchored in the past. It allows us to engage fully with life, to form healthier relationships, and to open our hearts to new experiences.

> In the words of Martin Luther King Jr., "Forgiveness is not an occasional act, it is a constant attitude."

When we forgive we assert our power, our joy, and our peace. We create space for love, understanding, and kindness to blossom in our hearts. We allow healing to occur, transforming our wounds into wisdom, our pain into power. Let this attitude of forgiveness guide us on our healing journey, leading us toward freedom, peace, and the full expression of our Divine Feminine energy.

The power of forgiveness is transformative. It's a key that unlocks the doors of our emotional prison, a balm that soothes our wounds, a bridge that leads us toward healing and freedom. As we continue to explore the path of emotional healing, let's remember to pack this powerful tool in our toolkit. Let's cultivate an attitude of forgiveness, towards ourselves and others, and let it guide us on our journey towards healing, growth, and the embodiment of the Divine Feminine.

This is my wish for you. This is the power of forgiveness.

Tools for Emotional Release

Journaling for Emotional Release

Emotions are like water flowing in a river – constantly flowing through us. When allowed to flow freely, it runs smoothly, carrying with it leaves, pebbles, and other debris. But when obstructed, the water builds up, creating pressure and potentially leading to a destructive flood. Similar to the river, when our emotions are expressed and acknowledged, they can flow and dissipate. But when suppressed or ignored, they can build up, leading to emotional overwhelm or even physical symptoms.

The act of writing can be profoundly therapeutic. It's like having a conversation with your inner self, a dialogue that can bring clarity, peace, and healing. Journaling serves as a channel through which our emotional river can flow freely. It provides a safe, non-judgmental space to express our feelings, fears, hopes, and dreams.

To use journaling for emotional release, start by creating a calm, quiet space where you won't be disturbed. Choose a journal that appeals to you and a writing instrument that you enjoy using. Begin to write, letting your thoughts flow freely. Don't worry about grammar, punctuation, or sentence structure. The purpose here is to express, not impress.

You can write about your day, about a situation that's been bothering you, or about your dreams for the future. You can ask yourself questions like, "What am I feeling right now?" or "What do I need right now?" and write down whatever comes to mind. Remember, this is your private space, where you can be honest, raw, and uncensored.

Alternatively, you might discover greater efficacy in expressing your thoughts verbally rather than through writing. Embrace the freedom of spontaneous verbalization, akin to the flow of stream of consciousness. Numerous recording apps facilitate the capturing of your spoken words. Subsequently, listening to the recordings offers an opportunity for reflection, allowing you to hear yourself articulate a unique perspective and creating space for the thoughts to transition from within you.

Breathwork for Emotional Healing

Breathwork, the practice of using conscious and controlled breathing techniques, is a powerful tool for emotional healing. It can help release stored emotions, reduce stress, and promote relaxation and emotional well-being.

One simple yet effective breathwork technique is deep abdominal breathing. Sit or lie down in a comfortable position. Place one hand on your chest and the other on your abdomen. Take a slow, deep breath in through your nose, allowing your abdomen to rise as you fill your lungs with air. Exhale slowly through your mouth, letting your abdomen fall. Continue this deep, rhythmic breathing for several minutes, focusing your attention on the rise and fall of your abdomen.

As you engage in breathwork, you might experience a range of emotions. You might feel a sense of calm and relaxation, or you might feel a surge of emotion as repressed feelings come to the surface. Whatever you experience, know that it's okay. Allow yourself to feel whatever comes up, without judgment or resistance.

Emotional Freedom Technique (EFT)

The Emotional Freedom Technique, also known as EFT or tapping, is a self-healing method that combines elements of traditional Chinese medicine and modern psychology. It involves tapping on specific acupressure points while focusing on a particular issue or emotion.

EFT has been shown to reduce stress, anxiety, and emotional distress. It works on the premise that all negative emotions are a disruption in the body's energy system. By tapping on the acupressure points, we can clear these disruptions, releasing the associated negative emotions.

To practice EFT, start by identifying the issue or emotion you'd like to work on. Rate the intensity of this issue or emotion on a scale of 0 to 10, with 10 being the most intense. Next, create a setup statement that acknowledges the problem and affirms self-acceptance, such as "Even though I feel anxious, I deeply and completely accept myself."

While repeating your setup statement, tap on the side of your hand (the karate chop point). Then, tap on the remaining points (top of the head, eyebrow, side of the eye, under the eye, under the nose, chin, collarbone, under the arm) while focusing on your issue or emotion. After a few rounds of tapping, reassess the intensity of your issue or emotion.

H'oponopono Prayer

Ho'oponopono is a traditional Hawaiian practice of reconciliation and forgiveness, rooted in the belief that healing occurs through the restoration of harmony and balance within oneself and with others. The practice involves repeating four simple phrases: *"I'm sorry. Please forgive me. Thank you. I love you."* These phrases are uttered with sincerity and intention, acknowledging one's responsibility for the disharmony and expressing a genuine desire for reconciliation and healing. My mentor shared this with me when I was going through a very difficult time of divorce and legal issues. I was at the point of feeling overwhelmed, anxious, and helpless. The repetition of this prayer did help anchor me in this time. When I had to go to a custody trial and was being questioned on the stand, I mentally vibrated this prayer.

Ho'oponopono emphasizes the interconnectedness of all beings and the power of forgiveness to release negative emotions and restore inner peace. It has been adapted into a modern spiritual practice for personal growth, healing, and transformation, spreading its message of love, forgiveness, and reconciliation across cultures and continents.

Journaling, breathwork, EFT, and prayer are effective tools for emotional release. They provide avenues for expressing and releasing emotions, promoting emotional healing and well-being. As we continue our journey of emotional healing, let's employ these tools, letting them guide us toward release, healing, and the full embodiment of our Divine Feminine energy.

Building Resilience and Inner Strength

Understanding the Nature of Resilience

Resilience, the capacity to bounce back from adversity, is often likened to a bamboo tree. Despite being slender and flexible, the bamboo tree is incredibly resilient. It can sway with the wind, even in the most violent storms, and yet it doesn't break. It can bend, but it doesn't easily snap. This ability to bend but not break, to sway but not fall, is the essence of resilience.

Resilience is not about avoiding difficulties or bypassing pain. It's about facing challenges head-on, enduring hardships, and emerging stronger. It's about learning from adversities, adapting to changes, and growing despite setbacks. It's about cultivating inner strength, not just to withstand the storms of life, but to thrive amidst them.

Strategies for Building Inner Strength

Building inner strength is like building physical strength. It requires regular practice, consistent effort, and time. Here are some strategies to help you build your inner strength:

- Cultivate a Positive Mindset: Look for the silver lining in every situation. Practice gratitude, focus on solutions rather than problems, and surround yourself with positive influences.

- Practice Self-Care: Take care of your physical, emotional, and mental health. Regular exercise, a balanced diet, sufficient sleep, stress management techniques, and positive social interactions can go a long way in enhancing your inner strength.

- Set and Achieve Goals: Setting and achieving goals can boost your confidence and determination. Start with small, achievable goals, and gradually work your way up to bigger ones.

- Foster Healthy Relationships: Surround yourself with people who uplift and support you. Cultivate relationships that are based on mutual respect, understanding, and positivity.

- Seek Support When Needed: It's okay to ask for help when you're struggling. Reach out to a trusted friend, family member, or mental health professional. Remember, seeking support is not a sign of weakness, but a testament to your strength and resilience.

Cultivating a Resilient Mindset

A resilient mindset is one that views challenges as opportunities for growth, that focuses on solutions rather than problems, that embraces change rather than resisting it. Cultivating such a mindset can significantly enhance your resilience and inner strength.

Here are a few strategies to cultivate a resilient mindset:

- Practice Positive Affirmations: Positive affirmations are statements that can help you challenge and overcome self-sabotaging thoughts. Repeat affirmations like "I am resilient," "I can handle whatever comes my way," "I am capable and strong" or "I love you, but I love me more."

- Embrace Change: Change is a natural part of life. Instead of resisting it, learn to embrace it. See it as an opportunity for growth and learning. It's okay to ride the wave of uncertainty.

- Cultivate Gratitude: Gratitude can shift your focus from what's wrong to what's right. Practice daily gratitude by pausing more often throughout the day and expressing 1 thing you are grateful for in that moment.

- Practice Mindfulness: Mindfulness can help you stay centered and calm, even in the face of adversity. Practice mindfulness through meditation, yoga, or simply focusing on your breath.

Building resilience and inner strength is a vital aspect of emotional healing. It equips us with the courage to face our emotional wounds, the endurance to navigate the healing process, and the strength to emerge from it stronger and wiser. As we continue our journey of emotional healing, in the next chapter let us explore physical movement to release emotions and move them through us.

Chapter Eight

The Divine Feminine: Dancing with Grace, Flowing with Life

As a gentle breeze stirs the leaves on a tree, so does the rhythm of music stir the soul within us. It awakens a primal instinct, a desire to move, to sway, to dance. Dancing, an ancient form of expression and communication, is a pure manifestation of the Divine Feminine. It embodies the fluidity, grace, and power that lies within each of us, inviting us to express ourselves in a language that transcends words. For me, dancing is how I come home to my body. It is my medicine every day.

In this chapter, we will explore the transformative power of dance as a conduit for expressing the Divine Feminine. We will delve into different dance styles, the therapeutic benefits of dance, and the role of dance in emotional release. Get ready to put on your dancing shoes and twirl to the rhythm of your heart!

The Dance of the Divine: Embodying Feminine Grace

Exploring Different Dance Styles

Dance is a universal language, understood and spoken by all cultures across the world. Each dance style, much like a dialect, brings its unique flavor and charm, telling a different story of the human experience.

- Belly Dancing: This Middle Eastern dance form emphasizes complex movements of the torso and is often associated with femininity and fertility. Its slow, fluid movements can help strengthen the core and improve flexibility, making it a wonderful dance style to embody the Divine Feminine.

- Contemporary Dance: A genre that emerged in the mid-20th century, contemporary dance is characterized by its versatility and improvisation. It encourages self-expression and emotional exploration, making it a great platform for the Divine Feminine to take center stage.

- Salsa: Originating from Latin America, Salsa is a high-energy dance form known for its lively rhythm and dynamic footwork. Dancing Salsa not only provides a great cardio workout but also helps build confidence - a key aspect of the Divine Feminine.

- Bharatanatyam: An ancient Indian classical dance, Bharatanatyam is known for its grace, purity, tenderness, and sculpturesque poses. The dance form is the embodiment of music in visual form, a ceremony, and an act of devotion.

- Sensual/Erotic Dancing: Sensual dancing, with its roots deeply embedded in cultural traditions and human expression, captivates the soul and ignites the senses. Originating from various corners of the globe, sensual dance forms have evolved over centuries, intertwining history, emotion, and movement into a mesmerizing tapestry of rhythm and grace. From the passionate tango of Argentina to the seductive sway of Middle Eastern belly dance, each style carries its own unique narrative, reflecting the spirit and essence of its people. Sensual dancing transcends mere physical motion; it is an intimate dialogue between body and music, a language of desire and connection.

- Somatic Dance: Somatic dance is a form of movement practice that focuses on experiencing the body from within, emphasizing internal bodily sensations, awareness, and connectivity. In somatic dance, the emphasis is not solely on external choreography or performance, but rather on exploring and expressing movement from a deep understanding of one's own body.

- Ecstatic Dance: Ecstatic dance is a form of free-form movement and expression that encourages individuals to let go of inhibitions and connect with their inner selves and the music. Dancers are invited to move spontaneously, without any set choreography, allowing their bodies to flow naturally to the rhythm and beat of the music. It's a practice that emphasizes self-expression, mindfulness, and personal exploration.

Remember, the aim is not to master these dance forms but to experience the joy of movement, the liberation of self-expression, and the embodiment of the Divine Feminine. So, give yourself the permission to explore, to experiment, and most importantly, to enjoy the process.

Dance as a Form of Self-Expression

Dance has been used as a form of self-expression for centuries. It offers us a platform to communicate our emotions, our experiences, and our very essence in a way words often fall short.

When we dance, we tell a story. A story of our joys and sorrows, our triumphs and struggles, our dreams and desires. Each movement, each gesture, each step is a word, a sentence, a paragraph in this story. And as we dance, we not only tell our story, but we also embrace it, own it, and celebrate it.

Dance also allows us to express the Divine Feminine within us. As we sway our hips, extend our arms, or twirl around, we embody the grace, the power, and the fluidity of the Divine Feminine. We become a living, breathing, dancing manifestation of the Goddess within us.

Dance for Emotional Release

Dance, in its purest form, is emotion in motion. It's a safe, non-verbal outlet for emotional release. When we dance, we allow our emotions to flow through us, to express themselves in movement, and to be released into the space around us.

As Martha Graham, a pioneer of modern dance, once said, "Dance is the hidden language of the soul." So, let your soul speak. Let it express its deepest emotions, its rawest feelings, its untold stories. And as you do so, you'll find a sense of release, a lightening of your emotional burden, a step closer to healing and wholeness.

In the tender embrace of dance, I've discovered a sacred sanctuary where my divine feminine essence blooms into artistry and creation. Through every fluid movement and rhythmic sway, I've surrendered to the raw beauty within, allowing it to blossom into a tapestry of expression that I now share with the world.

This journey isn't just about movements and choreography; it's a deeply personal odyssey of self-discovery and healing. Each motion is a whispered conversation with my soul, a gentle reminder of the profound connection between body, mind, and spirit. In the embrace of dance, I've found solace, liberation, and a profound sense of belonging—a homecoming to my body like no other.

As I weave through the intricate rhythms of life, I've learned to honor the scars and the stories they hold, allowing them to fuel my movement with authenticity and grace. Through dance, I've surrendered to my sovereignty, embracing vulnerability as a source of strength and resilience.

Sharing this journey with the world isn't just an act of performance—it's an offering of vulnerability, an invitation for others to embark on their own path of self-discovery and healing. In the sacred space of movement, I've found my voice, my truth, and the courage to share it with the world.

Yoga Poses for Balancing Feminine Energy

Yoga, a practice steeped in ancient wisdom, offers a unique avenue to connect with and balance our feminine energy. Certain yoga poses, or asanas, are particularly powerful in awakening this dormant strength.

Consider the elegance of the Moon Salutation, or Chandra Namaskar, a sequence that honors the nurturing lunar energy. Its gentle, fluid movements mirror the qualities of the Divine Feminine, promoting introspection and tranquility. Keep in mind there are many variations of this sequence, and I am sharing one of my favourites.

Start in mountain pose, feet firmly planted and hands in prayer position in front of your chest. Inhale and exhale.

Mountain Pose with hands in prayer position

Inhale arms up overhead, exhale and side bend to the right.

Side Bend

Inhale back up to straight position, exhale, opening legs up into goddess pose.

Goddess Pose

From goddess pose, inhale and raise arms parallel to the floor, palms facing down, reaching out to the sides. Exhale and engage your core muscles as you extend your torso to the right, hinging at your right hip.

Triangle Side Stretch, up reaching up

Then inhale stretching that arm up, exhale and bring that arm down to your foot, ankle, or shin feeling the stretch in the back of that right leg.

Triangle side stretch

Pivot that right foot forward and come down into a forward lunge with your right leg in front. Inhale arms overhead and exhale, hold the position.

Lunge with arms overhead

Inhale pivoting that foot to come into a side lunge on the right side. Exhale.

Side low lunge

Inhale coming into a yoga squat, exhale as you use your elbows against your knees to push your chest out.

Yoga Squat

Now you can continue the sequence on the left side. Flow into the side low lunge on the left side.

Side low lunge on left side.

Inhale and exhale as you pivot that left foot and turn your body into a forward lunge with left leg in front. Inhale arms overhead. Exhale as you come into triangle pose on the left.

Forward lunge on left side

Inhale as you gracefully bring your left hand down to your left shin, ankle, or the floor outside of your foot. Exhale keeping your legs strong and engaged.

Triangle pose on left side

Inhale stretching your left arm overhead and opening up your chest. Exhale as you wind slowly out of this posture and bring your torso back up to standing.

Triangle on left side with left arm extended.

Inhale and bend your knees and come into a wide squat into goddess pose. Exhale as you hold.

Goddess Pose

Inhale your legs together and stand straight. Exhale into a side bend to the left.

Side bend to the left

Finish the sequence and come back into Mountain pose with your hands in prayer position in front of your chest.

Mountain Pose

The number of times you repeat the Moon Salutation can vary based on your preference, energy level, and duration of your practice. As a general guideline, you can start with performing 3 to 5 runs to gradually warm up your body, sychonrize your breath and movement, and cultivate a sense of calmness. If you have more time and energy, you can increase the number of rounds accordingly up to 10 rounds or more.

Listen to your body and maintain mindfulness throughout the practice. Pay attention to your breath, alignment, and sensations in the body as your move through each round.

Another powerful asana is the Goddess Pose, or Deviasana. As the name suggests, this pose channels the strength and power of the divine feminine. It opens the heart and hips, sites often associated with emotional storage, promoting release and healing.

Goddess Pose

Variation: Goddess Pose on toes

Goddess Pose Variation with arms overhead

Baddha Konasana, or Bound Angle Pose, is another pose that beautifully stimulates the sacral chakra, the energy center associated with our emotions and sensuality. This pose, coupled with slow, deep breaths, can help to unlock and balance feminine energy. Feel free to support your knees with blocks underneath or a strap around your knees and hold the ends in your hands.

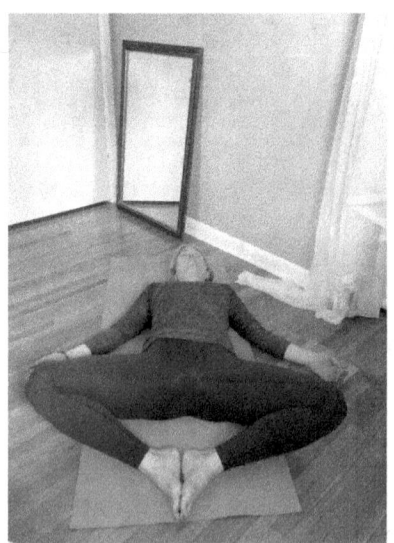

Bound Angle Pose

Remember, it's not about perfecting these poses but about the feeling and intention behind them. As you hold each pose, visualize the nurturing feminine energy flowing through your body, soothing, healing, and empowering you.

The Role of Breath in Yoga

Breath, or Pranayama in yogic terms, is a vital component of the yoga practice. The breath not only nourishes our bodies with life-giving oxygen, but also serves as a bridge between our physical and mental states.

In yoga, we use the breath as a tool to cultivate mindfulness, to anchor ourselves in the present, and to guide our movements. Each inhalation invites fresh energy and inspiration, while each exhalation allows us to release tension and surrender to the pose.

Consider Ujjayi breath, a pranayama technique often used in yoga. Known as the "ocean breath" for the sound it creates, Ujjayi breath involves constricting the back of the throat while breathing in and out through the nose. The result is a soothing, rhythmic breath that not only enhances focus and calm but also builds inner heat to cleanse and purify the body.

As you engage in your yoga practice, I encourage you to bring attention to your breath. Notice the rhythm, depth, and texture of your breath. Use it as a barometer of your internal state, guiding you to move with grace and ease.

Incorporating Meditation into Your Yoga Practice

Meditation, the practice of focusing the mind to achieve mental clarity and emotional calm, is a natural complement to yoga. Together, they create a harmonious symphony of mind-body integration, fostering a deep sense of inner balance and peace.

You could begin your yoga practice with a brief meditation, setting an intention for your practice. This could be a word or phrase that embodies your desired state or focus, such as "peace," "strength," or "self-love." As you move through your practice, keep returning to this intention, using it as an anchor for your mind.

You could also incorporate meditation at the end of your practice, during Savasana or corpse pose. As you lay still on your mat, turn your focus inward. Observe the sensations in your body, the rhythm of your breath, the thoughts flowing through your mind. Let them be, without judgment or attachment.

In this quiet stillness, you create a space for the Divine Feminine to surface. A space for introspection, for healing, for a deep sense of connection with your inner self.

As you continue your exploration of yoga, I invite you to incorporate these elements into your practice. Embrace the asanas that resonate with you, use your breath as a guide, and weave in moments of meditation. As you do so, may you experience the harmony, strength, and grace of the Divine Feminine.

Embracing Your Sensuality

Understanding the Difference Between Sensuality and Sexuality

In the vast tapestry of human experience, sensuality and sexuality are two threads that often intertwine, yet each holds its unique color and texture. Sexuality, with its vibrant hues, relates to sexual attraction, sexual activities, and sexual orientation. It is an integral part of our identity, shaping our relationships and our interactions.

Sensuality, on the other hand, paints with softer, subtler shades. It is not confined to sexual experiences but extends to all experiences that involve the senses. It is about savoring the velvety texture of a rose petal, the intoxicating aroma of freshly brewed coffee, the soothing melody of a raindrop hitting the window. It is about fully immersing ourselves in the symphony of sensations that life offers us.

In the context of the Divine Feminine, sensuality is a celebration of our physical existence, a testament to our ability to experience and relish the world around us. It fosters a deep connection with our bodies, enhancing our self-awareness, self-love, and overall well-being.

Sensual Practices for Self-Love

Engaging in sensual practices can be a profoundly self-nurturing experience. It's like whispering sweet words of love to your body, acknowledging its beauty, its capabilities, its sensations. Here are a few practices to guide you on this path:

- Mindful Bathing: Transform your daily bathing ritual into a mindful practice. Pay attention to the sensation of water cascading down your body, the fragrance of your bath products, the softness of your towel. Allow this practice to be a daily reminder of your commitment to self-love.

- Sensory Eating: Turn your meals into a sensory experience. Notice the color, texture, and aroma of your food. Take small bites, savoring the flavors that explode in your mouth. This practice not only enhances your enjoyment of food but also promotes mindful eating.

- Aroma Therapy: Scents can have a powerful impact on our mood and emotions. Light a scented candle, use an essential oil diffuser, or wear a perfume that makes you feel good. As you inhale the aroma, let it soothe your senses and uplift your spirit.

- Nature Walks: Nature offers an abundance of sensory experiences. Go for a walk in a park, beach, or forest. Feel the breeze on your skin, listen to the birds chirping, and smell the earthy scent of the forest. Let nature's symphony serenade your senses.

- Self-Touch: Through gentle caresses, tender embraces, and soothing strokes, self-touch becomes a conduit for self-compassion and self-awareness. It's a language of love spoken through fingertips, a reminder that we are worthy of our own affection and tenderness.

Remember, these practices are not about achieving a particular outcome, but about immersing yourself in the process, celebrating your senses, and honoring your body. As you engage in these practices, you're not only nurturing your body but also nourishing your soul, fostering a deep sense of self-love and self-acceptance.

If you desire more guidance, I have a free 3-day video series on Pelvic Freedom. Day 3 is a guided self-touch practice with yours truly. You can get it at this link. https://www.heateronhealth.com/pages/pelvicfreedom

Sensuality and Body Acceptance

Our bodies are the vessels that house our souls, the canvas where our life stories unfold, the temple of the Divine Feminine. Yet, many of us struggle with body acceptance. We judge our bodies, criticize them, and wish they were different. But embracing our sensuality can pave the way to body acceptance.

When we engage in sensual practices, we shift our focus from how our body looks to how it feels, from its appearance to its sensations. We start to appreciate our body for its abilities, its resilience, and its capacity for pleasure. We begin to see our body not as an object to be judged, but as a subject to be experienced.

As we cultivate this sensual connection with our bodies, we foster a sense of body acceptance. We learn to love our bodies, not for their size, shape, or color, but for their uniqueness, their beauty, their divinity. We learn to honor our bodies as the sacred abode of the Divine Feminine, deserving of love, respect, and care.

In the dance of life, sensuality invites us to move with grace, to flow with the rhythm, to express our emotions. It invites us to savor the symphony of sensations, to celebrate the joy of embodiment, to honor the divinity within us. As we embrace our sensuality, we not only enhance our connection with the Divine Feminine, but we also deepen our connection with ourselves, with our bodies, with the world around us. So, dear reader, I invite you to embrace your sensuality, to indulge your senses, to celebrate your body. As you do so, may you experience the beauty, the joy, and the power of the Divine Feminine, resonating within you and all around you.

Movement as Meditation

The Concept of Flow in Movement

Picture a leaf floating down a stream. It doesn't resist the current, doesn't struggle against the flow. Instead, it rides the waves, twists and turns, and moves with fluidity and ease. This concept of 'flow' in movement is a profound embodiment of the Divine Feminine. It's about letting go of control, embracing the rhythm of the body, and surrendering to the dance of life.

When we move with flow, we enter a state of heightened focus and immersion in the activity. Our movements become instinctive, spontaneous, and harmonious. We become one with our body, fully absorbed in the sensations, losing track of time and space. It's in this state of flow that movement transforms into meditation, a moving mantra that anchors us in the present and aligns us with our inner rhythm.

Mindful Movement Practices

Submerging into the realm of mindful movement, we find a plethora of practices that can guide us toward this state of flow. These practices invite us to experience movement not as a means to an end, but as an end in itself. They encourage us to step off the treadmill of routine and step onto the dance floor of mindfulness.

One such practice is Tai Chi, an ancient Chinese martial art often described as 'meditation in motion'. Tai Chi involves slow, flowing movements coupled with deep breathing, promoting a sense of calm and balance.

Walking meditation is another mindful movement practice that can be easily incorporated into everyday life. It involves walking slowly and mindfully, fully aware of each step, each breath, and each sensation.

Dance meditation, such as Ecstatic Dance, encourages free-form movement to music, fostering a sense of liberation, joy, and connection with one's body.

Sensual Somatic ™ is a dance practice deeply profound for me. I completed my facilitator certification in this mindful dance form that focuses on yoga foundational movements and weaves in exploration and expression through spinal undulations, hip circulations, twerking, and erotic dance. The aim is to slow down and deeply create awareness of subtle sensations and how your body moves through space.

Regardless of the practice you choose, the key is to remain fully present, to tune into your body's sensations, and to move with awareness and intention. As you engage in mindful movement, let it become a dance of the Divine Feminine, a dance of fluidity, grace, and power.

Movement and Emotional Release

Our bodies are not just vessels for our souls; they're also containers for our emotions. When we experience intense emotions, our bodies often store these feelings, leading to tension, discomfort, or even physical pain. Movement offers a pathway for releasing these stored emotions, freeing us from their grip, and restoring our emotional balance.

Think of a toddler throwing a tantrum. They stomp their feet, flail their arms, and let out a loud wail. Once the tantrum is over, they return to their playful, joyful selves, the emotional storm having passed. We, too, can use movement to express and release our emotions, to shake off our emotional dust, and to restore our inner equilibrium.

This could involve shaking your body vigorously to release pent-up stress, stomping your feet to let out frustration, or swaying gently to soothe anxiety. It could be a wild, passionate dance to express anger, a slow, graceful dance to express sadness, or a lively, energetic dance to express joy.

Remember, there's no right or wrong way to move. The aim is not to perform a perfect routine, but to express your authentic feelings. So, give yourself the freedom to move, to feel, to release. And as you do so, may you experience the power of movement as meditation, the joy of dancing with the Divine Feminine, and the liberation of emotional release.

In the divine rhythm of life, every heartbeat is a drumbeat, every breath is a melody, and every movement is a dance. As we move to this rhythm, we become dancers in the grand performance of life, embodying the grace, the fluidity, and the passion of the Divine Feminine. So, let's dance, dear reader. Let's move with intention, express with authenticity, and flow with life. As we do so, may we experience the transformative power of the Divine Feminine, guiding us, empowering us, and dancing with us - every step of the way.

Chapter Nine

Manifesting with the Divine Feminine: Turning Dreams into Reality

In this chapter, we will explore manifesting from the perspective of the Divine Feminine. We will delve into the Law of Assumption, the power of intention, and the role of emotions in manifestation. As we navigate through these topics, may you find the insights and tools to harness the power of manifestation, turning your dreams into reality.

Understanding Manifestation

The Law of Assumption

The Law of Assumption is a universal principle that posits that assumptions, beliefs, and imaginal acts shape our reality. It suggests that what we assume to be true, whether consciously or unconsciously, manifests in our experience. Think of it as planting seeds in a garden: the assumptions we nurture within ourselves grow into the reality we experience. Similarly, when we assume a certain state or outcome to be true, we set in motion the process of its manifestation.

This principle is at the heart of manifestation. By consciously assuming the reality of our desired outcomes, we can align ourselves with the experiences we wish to attract. However, it's important to remember that the Law of Assumption requires more than mere wishful thinking. It necessitates *embodying* the state of the wish fulfilled, believing in its inevitability, and persisting in that assumption until it materializes.

As we continue to explore manifestation in this chapter, reflect on this quote from Neville Goddard:

> Change your conception of yourself and you will automatically change the world in which you live. Do not try to change people; they are only messengers telling you who you are. Revalue yourself and they will confirm the change."

The Power of Intention

Intention is the driving force behind manifestation. It is the conscious decision to adopt a specific assumption or desired state as true. When we set an intention, we declare to ourselves and the universe what reality we are choosing to create. For instance, by embodying the essence of Loving Woman, my interactions naturally reflect this state, thereby influencing my communication and actions positively. As a result, embracing this quality has transformed and enriched my relationships, including those in romantic, familial, and parental contexts.

Setting an intention involves more than simply stating a desire; it requires embodying the feeling of the wish fulfilled and assuming the reality of its manifestation. It's like planting a seed in fertile soil, nurturing it with belief and expectation until it blossoms into fruition.

However, intention alone is not enough. It needs to be supported by faith, imagination, and persistence. We must have faith in the inevitability of our desired outcome, imagine ourselves living in the reality of that outcome, and persist in that assumption despite any apparent obstacles or challenges. This brings us to the next aspect of manifestation - the role of emotions.

The Role of Emotions in Manifestation

Emotions play a crucial role in the process of manifestation. They are the fuel that powers our assumptions and intentions. When we feel the emotions associated with our desired outcome - whether it be joy, satisfaction, or gratitude - we imbue our assumptions with the vibrational energy necessary for manifestation.

Imagine you want to manifest a new job. Rather than simply visualizing the job or repeating affirmations, immerse yourself in the emotions you would feel if you already had that job. Feel the excitement of embarking on a new adventure, the satisfaction of utilizing your skills and talents, and the gratitude for the opportunities that come your way. This is where you can imagine a scene that implies you have your desired job. This could be as simple as hearing a close friend or loved one saying "Congratulations!" Pay attention to how you feel when you imagine hearing this. These emotions infuse your assumptions with the vibrational frequency needed to attract your desired outcome.

Moreover, emotions serve as feedback about our alignment with our desires. Positive emotions indicate alignment, while negative emotions signal a need for adjustment. By tuning into our emotions, we can refine our assumptions and intentions to better align with our desired outcomes.

Understanding manifestation involves exploring the Law of Assumption, the power of intention, and the role of emotions. It's about recognizing our creative power and learning to use it consciously to manifest our desires. We are not mere spectators in the theater of life. We are the scriptwriters, directors, and lead actors in our own life story. We have the power to shape our experiences, manifest our dreams, and create a life that resonates with the wisdom and beauty of the Divine Feminine.

Aligning with Your Desires

Identifying Your True Desires

Our desires, like the North Star, guide us towards our destiny. They are the whispers of our soul, beckoning us towards experiences that resonate with our essence. But to follow these whispers, we must first learn to discern them.

Identifying your true desires is like sifting through a treasure chest filled with various gems, jewels, and treasures. Each item represents a desire or longing within you. Some gems may catch your eye immediately, sparkling brightly and drawing your attention effortlessly. These are like the desires that are clear and easily recognizable to you. However, as you continue to sift through the treasure chest, you may come across some items that are buried beneath layers of other treasures, perhaps obscured by doubts, fears, or societal expectations. These are like desires that may not be immediately apparent, requiring some introspection and self-awareness to uncover. It's about noticing the desires that stir your soul, that resonate with your essence. It's about distinguishing between the desires that are shaped by external influences - societal expectations, cultural norms, peer pressure - and those that spring from your inner self.

To identify your true desires, carve out some quiet time for introspection. Reflect on your dreams, your passions, your values. What makes your heart sing? What sets your soul on fire? What fills you with joy and fulfillment?

Record these reflections in a journal, using words, doodles, or whatever medium feels right. Allow your thoughts and feelings to flow freely, without judgment or censorship. Trust your intuition to guide you toward your true desires.

Exploring desires goes beyond simply reflecting on them; it involves actively engaging with them in the tangible world. Here are some ways to expand on that idea:

- **Try New Things**: Step out of your comfort zone and experiment with activities or experiences that pique your interest. Whether it's taking a dance class, trying new cuisine, or traveling to a new destination, giving yourself permission to explore different facets of life can uncover hidden passions and desires.

- **Seek Inspiration**: Surround yourself with sources of inspiration that align with your desires. This could include reading books, watching movies, listening to podcasts, or following individuals who embody the qualities or lifestyles you aspire to. Allow their stories and experiences to ignite your own passions and aspirations.

- **Connect with Others**: Engage in conversations with like-minded individuals who share similar desires or goals. Joining community groups, attending workshops, or participating in online forums can provide support, encouragement, and fresh perspectives on your journey of exploration.

- **Take Inspired Action**: Once you have identified your desires, take intentional steps towards manifesting them in your life. Break down larger goals into smaller, actionable tasks and commit to taking consistent steps forward. Trust in the process and remain open to the opportunities and synchronicities that arise along the way.

Remember that exploring desires is a journey of self-discovery and growth, and embracing the process with curiosity and openness can lead to profound transformation.

Aligning Your Thoughts and Feelings

Once you've identified your true desires, the next step is to align your thoughts and feelings with them. Imagine your desire as a destination and your imaginal acts as vehicles that transport you to that destination. When your thoughts and feelings are in alignment with your desires, they drive you towards your destination. When they're not in alignment, they steer you off course.

"With your desire defined, quietly go within and shut the door behind you. Lose yourself in your desire; feel yourself to be one with it; remain in this fixation until you have absorbed the life and name by claiming and feeling yourself to be and to have that which you desired. When you emerge from the hour of prayer you must do so conscious of being and possessing that which you heretofore desired."

—— **Neville Goddard,** Your Faith is Your Fortune

To align your thoughts with your desires, focus on positive, empowering thoughts that support your assumptions. Instead of thinking, "I can't do this," think, "I am capable and resourceful." Instead of thinking, "This is too hard," think, "I enjoy a good challenge." It's all about the attitude that you embody every day.

To align your feelings with your desires, cultivate the emotions you would feel if your desire were already fulfilled. If you desire to find a loving partner, cultivate feelings of love and companionship and consider that you already are a happy, loving woman in a loving, secure relationship. If you desire to achieve a career goal, cultivate feelings of accomplishment and fulfillment and adopt the identity of being a successful businesswoman now.

Remember, alignment is not a one-time task, but an ongoing process. It requires awareness, intention, and persistence. Get comfortable with these new desired states of being feeling awkward at the beginning. It's okay to be awkward. By consistently aligning your thoughts and feelings with your desires, you create a powerful momentum toward the manifestation of your desires.

Imagination

> "The great secret is a controlled imagination and a well-sustained attention firmly and repeatedly focused on the feeling of the wish fulfilled until it fills the mind and crowds all other ideas out of consciousness."
>
> —— **Neville,** The Power of Awareness

Focused imagination sessions serve as potent tools for manifestation, allowing us to immerse ourselves fully in the experience of our desired reality. During these sessions, we engage all of our senses to create a vivid and lifelike depiction of our wishes fulfilled.

So you are sitting in your chair, relaxed, and this is the perfect time to surrender to the power of your own human imagination. Close your eyes and take a deep breath, allowing yourself to relax into a state of receptivity. Now, feel as if your desired outcome has already come to fruition.

Perhaps, it is the financial freedom you are desiring. Rather than imagining how you make the money. Imagine a scene that implies your wish is fulfilled. Start from being in the state of "Financially Secure." What would you do if you felt financially secure? How would it change how you spend money at the grocery store or how you feel about it? How would it change how you talk about money? Maybe it would be a trip you take.

Engage your senses fully in this process. See the scene unfold before you with crystal clarity: visualize the details of your surroundings, the people involved, and the emotions you would experience in this moment of fulfillment. Imagine the colors, shapes, and textures vividly, painting a picture of your desired reality. It doesn't need to be a long drawn-out scene. It really could be quick and simple.

Next, tune into the sounds of this imagined scenario. Hear the voices, the laughter, the music, or the sounds of nature that accompany your wish fulfilled. Maybe it is hearing someone specific say something to you. Allow these auditory cues to deepen your immersion in the experience.

Now, focus on the sensations in your body. Feel the warmth of the sun on your skin, the softness of a loved one's touch, or the exhilaration of achieving your goal. Let these physical sensations anchor you in the present moment, reinforcing the reality of your desired outcome.

As you continue with your imagination session, tap into your sense of taste and smell. Imagine the aroma of your favorite meal wafting through the air, or the taste of a celebratory drink on your lips. Let these sensory experiences heighten your sense of anticipation and fulfillment.

Throughout this process, allow yourself to fully embody the emotions associated with your desired reality. Whether it's joy, gratitude, love, or excitement, let these feelings wash over you, filling you with a sense of empowerment and possibility.

By engaging all of your senses in these imagination sessions, you not only create a compelling vision of your desired reality but also signal to the universe your readiness to receive it. With each session, you reinforce your belief in the inevitability of your wish fulfilled, paving the way for its manifestation in your life.

Aligning with your desires involves identifying your true desires, aligning your thoughts and feelings with your desires, and using your imagination consciously. It's about tuning into the whispers of your soul, steering your thoughts and feelings in the direction of your desires, and painting a vivid mental picture of your desires fulfilled. As you practice these steps, you not only align with your desires but also tap into the transformative power of the Divine Feminine, turning your dreams into reality.

Practical Steps to Manifestation

Releasing Limiting Beliefs

Just as weeds can hinder the growth of plants in a garden, limiting beliefs can hinder the manifestation of our desires. They create mental blocks, distort our perception, and impede our progress. Releasing these limiting beliefs is like weeding the garden of our mind, creating space for our intentions to grow and thrive.

Identifying limiting beliefs is the first step towards releasing them. Notice your thoughts, especially those that make you doubt your ability to manifest your desires. Thoughts like "I'm not good enough," "I don't deserve this," or "This is too good to be true" are often signs of limiting beliefs.

Once you've identified your limiting beliefs, challenge them. Replace them with empowering beliefs that support your desires. For instance, instead of thinking "I'm not good enough," think "I am worthy and capable." Instead of thinking "I don't deserve this," think "I deserve all the good in my life." Go back to those embodied states. Would Loving Woman think she is not good enough? No. Loving Woman knows she is amazing and worthy now.

Remember, releasing limiting beliefs is a process. It requires awareness, patience, and persistence. But as you prune these mental weeds, you clear the path for your intentions, allowing them to blossom into beautiful manifestations of your desires.

Embracing Abundance

Understanding the Concept of Abundance

Nature is Wealth. Imagine standing in a vast meadow on a sunny day, the sky above you a brilliant blue, the earth beneath you teeming with life. Colorful wildflowers sway in the breeze, bees and butterflies flit from blossom to blossom, and birds sing from the treetops. Nature is a living portrait of abundance.

Abundance, in its essence, is a recognition of the plentiful nature of the universe. It's the realization that there is enough for everyone and that the universe is inherently generous and supportive. It's about viewing life not as a struggle for limited resources, but as a celebration of limitless possibilities.

In the context of manifestation, embracing abundance means trusting in the universe's capacity to fulfill our desires. It's about letting go of lack and limitation and aligning with the expansive energy of abundance. It's about welcoming prosperity, joy, and fulfillment into our lives, knowing that we are deserving of all the good the universe has to offer.

Shifting from a Scarcity to an Abundance Mindset

Now, picture yourself standing at the edge of a desert. The harsh sun beats down on the barren landscape, where water and life are scarce. This is the landscape of scarcity, a mindset that focuses on lack, competition, and survival.

A scarcity mindset is like a lens that distorts our view of the world. It makes us see life as a competition for limited resources, and makes us fear that there's not enough to go around. It breeds insecurity, jealousy, and anxiety, hindering our ability to manifest our desires.

Shifting from a scarcity to an abundance mindset is like trading the desert for the meadow. It's about changing the lens through which we view the world, focusing on abundance rather than lack. It's about celebrating others' successes, sharing generously, and trusting in the universe's abundance.

This shift requires awareness, practice, and patience. It involves challenging our scarcity-based beliefs, cultivating a sense of gratitude, and fostering an attitude of generosity. As we shift towards an abundance mindset, we open ourselves to the flow of prosperity, joy, and fulfillment, enhancing our manifestation power.

Cultivating an Attitude of Generosity

Have you ever noticed how giving a gift fills you with joy and fulfillment? Or how helping someone makes you feel good about yourself? This is the magic of generosity. When we give, we align with the energy of abundance, reinforcing our belief in the universe's generosity.

Generosity is not just about giving material things. It's about giving our time, our attention, our kindness. It's about sharing our knowledge, our skills, our love. It's about giving without expecting anything in return, knowing that the act of giving is its own reward.

Cultivating an attitude of generosity involves being mindful of the opportunities to give that present themselves each day. It could be as simple as giving a smile, a compliment, or a word of encouragement. It could be lending a listening ear, offering a helping hand, or sharing a meal.

As we cultivate generosity, we not only enrich others' lives but also our own. We invite abundance into our lives, foster a sense of connection, and enhance our manifestation power. In the words of Winston Churchill,

> "We make a living by what we get, but we make a life by what we give."

The dance of manifestation is a delicate balance of intention, emotion, and action. It's about aligning with our desires, cultivating positive emotions, and taking aligned action. It's about understanding the Law of Assumption, harnessing the power of intention, and using emotions as a manifestation tool. As we dance to the rhythm of manifestation, we not only turn our dreams into reality, but also invite abundance, joy, and fulfillment into our lives.

So, dear reader, let's dance. Let's play more. Let's manifest. Let's create a life that resonates with the wisdom and beauty of the Divine Feminine. As we move forward, may we remember that we are not just dancers in the grand performance of life, but also the choreographers of our own dance. We have the power to shape our experiences, manifest our dreams, and create a life that resonates with the wisdom and beauty of the Divine Feminine. May this understanding guide us, empower us, and inspire us as we continue our exploration of the Divine Feminine in the chapters ahead.

Chapter Ten

The Divine Feminine Sisterhood: United in Strength, Resilience and Love

Close your eyes for a moment and imagine you are in a bustling city, surrounded by skyscrapers that tower above you, reaching towards the heavens. The streets pulse with the energy of the people who walk them, each person with their own story, dreams, and aspirations. Some buildings are sleek and modern, others are historic and ornate, and yet others are adorned with vibrant street art. Despite their architectural differences, they coexist harmoniously, forming the vibrant tapestry of the urban landscape. This is the essence of sisterhood - a community of individuals, diverse yet interconnected, standing together in shared strength, resilience, and support amidst the bustling rhythm of city life.

In the realm of the Divine Feminine, sisterhood holds a special place. It is a sacred space of shared experiences and empathy, collective empowerment, and healing connections. It is a pillar of strength, a beacon of hope, and a source of comfort and inspiration. In this chapter, we will explore the power of sisterhood, delving into its various facets and understanding its role in our journey towards embracing the Divine Feminine.

The Power of Sisterhood

Shared Experiences and Empathy

Picture a group of women sitting in a circle, each sharing their story, their struggles, their victories. One woman speaks of her journey of self-discovery, another shares her experience of motherhood, and yet another talks about her battle with illness. As each woman speaks, the others listen with empathy, their hearts resonating with the shared human experience. This is the essence of sisterhood - a space where women can share their experiences, find validation, and feel heard and understood.

Sharing our experiences can be cathartic, allowing us to express our emotions, process our experiences, and gain insights. It can also help us realize that we are not alone in our struggles, that others have walked similar paths and faced similar challenges. This shared understanding fosters empathy, a deep sense of connection that transcends surface differences and touches the core of our common humanity.

Collective Empowerment

Nature is intelligent. With a flock of birds flying in a V formation, the bird in front leads the way, reducing the wind resistance for the birds behind it. When the leading bird tires, it moves to the back, allowing another bird to take the lead.

This cooperative behavior allows the flock to fly longer distances, demonstrating the power of collective empowerment.

In a similar vein, sisterhood is a powerful force for collective empowerment. When one woman rises, she lifts others with her; when one woman shines, she illuminates the path for others. This collective empowerment not only amplifies our individual strengths but also fosters a sense of unity, solidarity, and mutual support. It reminds us that we are stronger together, and that our collective power is greater than the sum of our individual powers.

The Healing Power of Connection

Think of a time when you were feeling low, and a friend reached out to you. Their kind words, their understanding nod, their comforting presence - didn't it make you feel better? This is the healing power of connection, a power that is amplified in the context of sisterhood.

Connecting with others, especially those who understand our experiences and empathize with our feelings, can have a profound healing effect. It can alleviate feelings of isolation and loneliness, provide emotional support, and foster a sense of belonging. In a sisterhood, this healing connection is nurtured and strengthened, providing a safe space for emotional expression, mutual support, and personal growth.

As we journey through life, embracing the Divine Feminine within us, the sisterhood serves as our tribe, our support system, and our guiding star. It reminds us that we are not alone, that we are part of a larger whole, interconnected and interdependent. It empowers us to rise, to shine, to thrive. And as we rise, we lift others with us, creating a ripple effect of empowerment, healing, and love. This, dear reader, is the power of sisterhood.

Creating Safe Spaces for Women

Establishing Trust and Confidentiality

Trust and confidentiality provide the nurturing environment for open communication, empathy, and unity to flourish and grow.

Building trust in a sisterhood involves consistency, honesty, and empathy. Consistency in our actions, words, and attitudes assures our sisters that we are reliable and dependable. Honesty, both in expressing our own emotions and in giving feedback to others, fosters authenticity and transparency. Empathy, the ability to understand and share the feelings of others, nurtures emotional connection and solidarity.

Confidentiality, the assurance that personal experiences and emotions shared within the group will not be disclosed to others, is another cornerstone of trust. It creates a safe container for vulnerability, allowing the members to share their experiences, fears, and aspirations without the fear of judgment or exposure. Establishing confidentiality involves setting clear guidelines about what can be shared outside the group and what should remain within the group, and ensuring that all members agree to and respect these guidelines.

The Sister Wound

The sister wound is a deep-seated pain rooted in the complexities of female relationships. It's the result of betrayals, competition, and unmet needs within sisterhood dynamics, often leaving emotional scars that hinder trust and connection. Whether born from jealousy, comparison, or unresolved conflicts, the sister wound can manifest as feelings of inadequacy, isolation, or even hostility towards other women. Healing this wound requires introspection, forgiveness, and a willingness to rebuild trust and solidarity among women. By acknowledging and addressing the sister wound with empathy and compassion, we can cultivate healthier, more supportive relationships that nurture growth and empowerment for all involved.

Encouraging Open Communication

Turning our gaze back to our garden metaphor, open communication is the sun that warms the garden, allowing the flowers to bloom in their full glory. In a sisterhood, open communication paves the way for mutual understanding, empathetic support, and collective growth.

Encouraging open communication begins with creating an environment where each member feels valued, heard, and understood. It involves active listening, where we give our undivided attention to the person speaking, reflecting back their thoughts and feelings, and refraining from interrupting or imposing our own opinions.

It also involves expressing our own thoughts and feelings honestly and respectfully. This can be facilitated by using "I" statements, which allow us to express our feelings without blaming or criticising others. For instance, instead of saying "You are wrong," we can say "I see things differently."

Moreover, open communication includes non-verbal communication. Paying attention to body language, facial expressions, and tone of voice can provide insights into unspoken emotions and needs, enhancing mutual understanding and empathy.

Fostering a Non-Judgmental Environment

Finally, a non-judgmental environment is the protective fence around our garden, shielding the delicate flowers from harsh winds and predators. In a sisterhood, a non-judgmental environment enables each woman to express herself freely, and to be her authentic self, without fear of judgment, criticism, or rejection.

Cultivating a non-judgmental environment involves conscious effort and practice. It starts with self-awareness, recognizing our own biases, prejudices, and judgments. It requires mindfulness, observing our thoughts and feelings without getting caught up in them. And it involves a commitment to acceptance, embracing each woman's unique experiences, perspectives, and identities.

In a non-judgmental environment, each woman is seen, heard, and valued for who she is, not who she 'should' be. Differences are respected, mistakes are seen as opportunities for learning, and each woman's unique journey is honored.

In conclusion, creating safe spaces for women involves establishing trust and confidentiality, encouraging open communication, and fostering a non-judgmental environment. These elements form the foundation of a robust sisterhood, a sanctuary where each woman can express her divine feminine power and contribute to the collective strength, resilience, and love of the group. Personally, I've been fortunate to be witnessed by sisters who are on similar journeys, and the safe space that was cultivated allowed me to share things I didn't share with anyone else. As we continue to explore the divine feminine in the chapters ahead, may we strive to create such safe spaces in our own lives, nurturing our own sisterhoods of strength, resilience, and love.

Supporting and Empowering Each Other

Active Listening and Validation

Imagine sitting across from a friend, her eyes welling up with tears as she shares a painful experience. You reach out, gently squeeze her hand, and say, "I see your pain, and I'm here for you." This simple act of active listening and validation can provide immense comfort, letting her know she's not alone.

Active listening is more than just hearing the words someone says. It's about being fully present, paying attention not only to their words but also their body language, their tone of voice, their unspoken emotions. It's about putting aside your own thoughts and judgments and immersing yourself in their experience. By doing so, you create a safe space for them to express their feelings, to feel seen and heard, to find solace and comfort.

Validation is the act of acknowledging and accepting someone's feelings. It's not about agreeing with them or sharing their perspective, but about respecting their emotions, their experiences, their truth. When we validate someone, we communicate a powerful message: "Your feelings matter. Your experiences are valid. You are worthy of respect and understanding."

By practicing active listening and validation, we can provide invaluable support to our sisters, strengthening our bonds of trust, empathy, and love. It's a testament to the power of the Divine Feminine, the nurturing, compassionate energy that lies within each of us.

Mutual Encouragement and Inspiration

Envision a group of women standing in a circle, holding hands, their faces glowing with warmth and admiration. One woman steps forward, and shares her dream of starting her own business. The others cheer her on, their words brimming with encouragement and positivity. This is the power of mutual encouragement and inspiration - a catalyst for dreams, a beacon of hope, a source of strength.

Mutual encouragement is about uplifting each other, cheering each other on, and believing in each other's capabilities. It's about speaking words of affirmation, expressing faith in each other's dreams, and celebrating each other's achievements. It's about being each other's cheerleaders, providing the motivation, confidence, and support needed to overcome obstacles and reach our goals.

Inspiration, on the other hand, is about igniting the spark of creativity and passion in each other. It's about sharing our experiences, our ideas, our insights, and kindling the fire of inspiration in each other's hearts. It's about learning from each other, drawing on each other's wisdom, and growing together.

By fostering mutual encouragement and inspiration, we not only support each other's dreams and aspirations but also empower each other to reach our fullest potential. It's a manifestation of the Divine Feminine, the powerful, transformative energy that propels us toward growth, fulfillment, and success.

Collaborative Problem-Solving

Picture a group of women gathered around a table, their brows furrowed in deep concentration, their minds buzzing with ideas. They're brainstorming solutions for a problem one of them is facing, pooling their collective wisdom, experience, and creativity. This is collaborative problem-solving - a testament to the power of unity, the strength of diversity, and the potential of collective intelligence.

Collaborative problem-solving involves working together to address a problem or challenge. It's about leveraging our collective strengths, perspectives, and expertise to find effective solutions. It's about listening to each other, respecting each other's ideas, and building on each other's contributions.

Collaborative problem-solving is not about finding 'the' solution, but about exploring 'possible' solutions. It's not about who's right and who's wrong, but about what works and what doesn't. It's about learning from each other, growing together, and transforming challenges into opportunities.

In the context of a sisterhood, collaborative problem-solving can be a powerful tool for personal growth and collective empowerment. It's a reflection of the Divine Feminine, the harmonious, collaborative energy that fosters unity, understanding, and collective progress.

Celebrating the Feminine Spirit

Honoring Individual Strengths and Achievements

In the magical dance of life, every woman pirouettes to the rhythm of her unique melody, her individual strengths and achievements forming the notes of her song. These strengths, whether they are resilience in the face of adversity, empathy that comforts others, creativity that paints the world in radiant colors, or any other quality, are feathers in her cap, symbols of her unique journey and personal growth.

In the nurturing ambiance of sisterhood, each woman's strengths are recognized, appreciated, and honored. It's like a beautiful garden where each flower is admired for its unique beauty, its vibrant colors, its intoxicating fragrance. Acknowledging and honoring individual strengths not only boosts self-confidence and self-esteem but also fosters mutual respect and appreciation.

Likewise, every achievement, big or small, is celebrated. It could be a personal milestone like overcoming a fear, achieving a health goal, or learning a new skill. Or a professional accomplishment like starting a business, getting a promotion, or completing a challenging project. Each achievement is a testament to her courage, determination, and resilience, deserving of recognition and celebration.

Celebrating Collective Milestones

Just as individual strengths and achievements are honored, so are collective milestones celebrated. The sisterhood rejoices in shared accomplishments, collective victories, and group progress. Whether it's the successful completion of a group project, the achievement of a shared goal, or the anniversary of the sisterhood, every collective milestone is a cause for celebration.

Celebrating collective milestones fosters a sense of unity, camaraderie, and mutual pride. It strengthens the bonds of sisterhood, enhancing the sense of belonging and togetherness. It's like a harmonious orchestra where each instrument contributes to the symphony, and the success of the symphony is shared by all.

Rituals and Ceremonies to Honor the Feminine

Rituals and ceremonies are powerful tools for honoring the Divine Feminine and celebrating the sisterhood. They are sacred acts that create a bridge between the physical and spiritual realms, providing a pathway for the Divine Feminine to flow into our lives.

These rituals and ceremonies can take many forms, depending on the beliefs, traditions, and preferences of the sisterhood. It could be a moon circle to connect with the lunar cycles and feminine energy, a gratitude ceremony to express appreciation for each other and the universe, a storytelling session to share experiences and wisdom, or any other ritual that resonates with the group.

Through these rituals and ceremonies, the sisterhood honors the Divine Feminine, celebrates their unity and diversity, and strengthens their connection with each other and the universe. They provide a sacred space to express, reflect, connect, and grow, fostering a deep sense of reverence, awe, and wonder.

In conclusion, the spirit of the Divine Feminine is celebrated in the sisterhood through honoring individual strengths and achievements, celebrating collective milestones, and conducting rituals and ceremonies. This celebration is a beautiful symphony of respect, appreciation, unity, and reverence, resonating with the rhythm of the Divine Feminine and echoing in the hearts of each woman in the sisterhood.

As we continue our exploration in the chapters ahead, may we carry this spirit of celebration in our hearts, letting it illuminate our path, inspire our actions, and enhance our connection with the Divine Feminine. May it remind us of the beauty, strength, and grace of being women, of the sacredness of our journey, and of the transformative power of the Divine Feminine.

Chapter Eleven

Divine Feminine: Embracing the Sacred in Everyday Life

Bringing the Divine Feminine into Your Daily Routine

Consider the warmth and comfort of returning home after a long day. As you step through the door, a sense of peace envelops you, like a familiar embrace. This feeling of home represents the Divine Feminine energy, a constant source of nurturing and support in your daily life. It is always present, offering solace and acceptance, waiting for you to come back, to find refuge, and to experience its comforting presence.

Morning Rituals to Connect with the Divine Feminine

The morning presents an opportunity to set the tone for the rest of your day. Just as the sun rises to fill the sky with its warm, radiant glow, you can rise to welcome the Divine Feminine into your day.

- Morning Meditation: Start your day with a short meditation. Find a quiet, comfortable spot. Close your eyes, take a few deep breaths, and visualize the Divine Feminine energy as a warm, golden light, flowing into you, filling you with love, strength, and serenity.

- Affirmations: Follow your meditation with positive affirmations. Stand in front of a mirror, look into your eyes, and repeat affirmations like "I am strong," "I am beautiful," and "I am divine." Feel the words resonate within you, reinforcing your connection with the Divine Feminine.

- Movement: Incorporate some gentle movement into your morning routine. It could be a few stretches, a yoga routine, or some freestyle ecstatic dancing. As you move, imagine the Divine Feminine energy flowing through you, guiding your movements, awakening your body.

- Nourishment: Nourish your body with a healthy, mindful breakfast. As you prepare your meal, infuse it with the intention of self-care, honoring your body as the temple of the Divine Feminine. As you eat, savor each bite, each flavor, each texture, expressing gratitude for the nourishment.

Incorporating Mindfulness into Daily Activities

Mindfulness, the practice of being fully present and engaged in the current moment, is a powerful way to connect with the Divine Feminine throughout your day.

- Work: Whether you're working in an office or at home, take short mindfulness breaks every hour or so. Pause, take a few deep breaths, and tune into your senses. Notice the sounds around you, the sensation of your body against the chair, the rhythm of your breath. This simple practice can help you stay centered and balanced, even amidst the busyness of work.

- Chores: Turn mundane chores into mindful practices. Whether you're washing dishes, doing laundry, or cleaning your home, bring your full attention to the task. Notice the sensation of the water against your skin as you wash the dishes, the rhythmic motion of folding laundry, the satisfaction of seeing a clean, tidy space. Infuse each task with the intention of creating a harmonious, nurturing environment for yourself and your loved ones.

- Leisure: Even during leisure activities, mindfulness can enhance your experience. Whether you're reading a book, watching a movie, or gardening, immerse yourself in the activity. Notice the words on the page as you read, the colors on the screen as you watch a movie, the feel of the earth beneath your hands as you garden. Allow each activity to become a celebration of the present moment, a dance with the Divine Feminine.

Evening Reflection and Gratitude Practice

As the day draws to a close, spend some time in quiet reflection and gratitude.
- Reflection: Reflect on the day's events, your emotions, your interactions. Without judgment, observe your experiences, learn from them, and let them go. As you release the day's experiences, visualize the Divine Feminine energy wrapping you in a warm, soothing blanket, preparing you for a restful night's sleep.

- Gratitude: End your day with a gratitude practice. Write down three things you're grateful for from the day. It could be a kind gesture from a stranger, a task you completed, or a beautiful sunset. As you express gratitude, you cultivate a mindset of abundance, attracting more experiences to be grateful for.

Incorporating the Divine Feminine into your daily routine doesn't require drastic changes or elaborate rituals. It's about infusing your everyday activities with mindfulness, intention, and a sense of sacredness. It's about turning ordinary moments into extraordinary experiences, each day into a beautiful dance with the Divine Feminine. As you embrace this practice, may you experience the joy, serenity, and fulfillment of living in harmony with the Divine Feminine.

The Role of Mindfulness

Mindfulness is akin to a gentle stream, its clear waters reflecting the world around it without distortion. Its serene flow invites us to be present, to observe without judgment, to engage with life in its purest form. Through mindful practices, we can attune ourselves to the rhythm of the present moment, inviting the Divine Feminine to flow through us with grace and ease.

Mindful Breathing

In the symphony of life, our breath is the steady drumbeat, the constant rhythm that anchors us in the present moment. Each inhalation invites fresh energy, each exhalation allows release, creating a harmonious flow of life force within us.

Mindful breathing is about tuning into this rhythm, observing the ebb and flow of our breath, and aligning our awareness with it. It's as simple as closing your eyes, placing a hand on your heart, and taking a few deep, conscious breaths.

As you inhale, feel your chest rise, your heart expand, your body fill with life-giving energy. As you exhale, feel your body relax, your mind calm, your spirit center. With each breath, anchor yourself more deeply in the present moment, aligning your awareness with your body, your environment, your inner self.

Mindful Movement

Life is a dance, a beautiful ballet choreographed by the Divine Feminine. Each movement, each gesture, each step is a word in the language of the body, expressing emotions, experiences, and energies.

Mindful movement is about immersing ourselves in this dance, being fully present in each twist, each turn, each leap. It's not about achieving a perfect form or following a specific routine. It's about moving with awareness, expressing authentically, and celebrating the joy of embodiment.

You could practice mindful movement through a gentle yoga flow, a spontaneous dance, or even a leisurely walk. As you move, tune into your body's sensations, noticing the stretch of your muscles, the alignment of your posture, the rhythm of your heart. Let each movement become a meditation, a sacred dance with the Divine Feminine.

Mindful Eating

Our relationship with food is a reflection of our relationship with life. It's an intimate communion with the earth, a celebration of the abundance of nature, a nurturing of our body and spirit.

Mindful eating is about bringing this awareness to our meals, transforming them from a routine task into a sacred ritual. It's not about following a strict diet or counting calories. It's about savoring each morsel, appreciating each flavor, and honoring the nourishment it provides.

As you prepare your meal, infuse it with love and gratitude. As you sit down to eat, create a calm, quiet environment. Take a moment to appreciate the colors, the aromas, and the textures of your food. As you take your first bite, close your eyes, savor the flavors, chew slowly, and swallow mindfully. Are you starting to understand that cultivating the Divine Feminine is essentially slowing down and attuning to subtle sensations and immersive experiences?

As we weave these mindful practices into the tapestry of our daily lives, we not only enhance our presence, awareness, and clarity, but also deepen our connection with the Divine Feminine. We learn to dance with life, to savor each moment, to honor our emotions and experiences. We learn to embrace the sacred in the ordinary, the divine in the mundane, the magic in the everyday.

Embracing Simplicity and Intention

Simplifying Your Physical Environment

There is something about a serene, tranquil lake on a calm morning that feels like home to me. The water is still, reflecting the sky above with perfect clarity. There's a sense of peace, of simplicity, of uncluttered beauty. A similar sense of tranquility can be achieved in our lives when we simplify our physical environment, creating a space that mirrors the calm, clear waters of the lake, embodying the essence of the Divine Feminine.

Start by assessing your living and working spaces. Are they cluttered with unnecessary items? Do they create a sense of chaos or calm? Are they filled with things that serve a purpose and bring you joy? If not, it's time to de-clutter.

Begin with one area at a time - a drawer, a shelf, a room. Handle each item and ask yourself, "Does this serve a purpose? Does it bring me joy?" If the answer is no, let it go. Donate it, recycle it, or discard it. Be ruthless in your pursuit of simplicity.

In this process, not only will you be creating a more peaceful, harmonious environment, but you'll also be making space for new things, new experiences, new energies to flow into your life. You'll be fostering a sense of calm and clarity, aligning your physical surroundings with the serene, tranquil energy of the Divine Feminine.

Embodying States of Being for Your Day

Imagine you're about to set out on a trip. Would you set out without a destination in mind? Or would you chart a route, set a destination, and travel accordingly?

Embodying intentional states of being for your day is like charting a route for your day. It gives direction to your thoughts, focus to your actions, and purpose to your day. It allows you to drive the car, your life, towards your desired goals, your dreams, your Divine Feminine essence.

Start each day by imagining a few things you want to happen and that you want to go well for that day. It could be as simple as enjoying a yummy meal with your loved one or feeling satisfied and accomplished after an important work meeting.

Take a few moments in the morning to imagine 5-7 things going well and working out for you. Let it set the tone for your thoughts, your actions, your choices. Let it be the compass that guides you through the day, aligning your daily voyage with the gentle, guiding light of the Divine Feminine.

Practicing Contentment

Picture a beautiful lotus flower, blooming in the midst of a muddy pond. Despite the mud, the murkiness, the chaos, the lotus remains untouched, its beauty undiminished. It does not wish to be anywhere else, to be anything else. It is content, at peace, in harmony with its environment.

Practicing contentment is like being the lotus in the pond. It's about finding peace amidst the chaos, joy amidst the challenges, harmony amidst the discord. It's about appreciating what you have, where you are, who you are, without constantly seeking more, better, different.

Begin by acknowledging the blessings in your life - the people who love you, the comforts you enjoy, the abilities you possess. Express gratitude for these blessings, allowing a sense of contentment to fill your heart.

Then, throughout the day, whenever you find yourself longing for something different, pause. Bring your attention back to the present moment, to what you have, to who you are. Remind yourself that you are enough, that you have enough.

Practicing contentment cultivates a sense of inner peace, a deep appreciation for life's simple pleasures, and a profound connection with the Divine Feminine. It allows you to bloom like the lotus, radiating beauty, serenity, and grace, no matter where you are planted.

Living Authentically: Recognizing and Honoring Your Feelings

In the symphony of life, our feelings are the notes that compose our unique melody. Each feeling, be it joy, sadness, anger, or peace, adds a distinctive tone, creating a harmonic blend that resonates with our authentic self. Recognizing and honoring these feelings is like tuning into our inner music, aligning our dance of life with the rhythm of our emotions.

Our feelings are our internal compass, guiding us towards experiences that align with our true selves, and warning us about situations that don't. They are our feedback mechanism, signaling when we are in harmony with our values and when we are off-track. They are our teachers, offering valuable lessons about ourselves, our relationships, and our world.

To recognize and honor your feelings, start by creating a 'feelings journal'. Each day, spend a few minutes jotting down the emotions you experienced and the situations that triggered them. Over time, you will notice patterns, gaining insights into your emotional landscape.

Then, cultivate emotional mindfulness. Throughout the day, pause to check in with your feelings. Tune into your body, your heart, your gut. What emotions are present? Are they comfortable or uncomfortable? What messages are they conveying?

Finally, practice emotional self-care. When you're feeling joy, savor it, amplify it. When you're feeling pain, comfort yourself, and seek support. When you're feeling angry, express it constructively, and release it. Honor your feelings, without judgment, without suppression, with compassion and understanding. Let emotions be visitors and flow through you and realize they don't have to define you.

Expressing Your Truth

Imagine standing on a mountaintop, calling out into the vast expanse, your voice echoing back to you. This is your truth, your unique voice, your authentic expression. Embodying the Divine Feminine involves finding this voice and having the courage to express it.

Your truth is your personal narrative, your unique perspective, your core beliefs. It's the essence of who you are, shaped by your experiences, your values, your dreams. Expressing your truth is about communicating this essence, authentically, honestly, courageously.

To express your truth, start by defining it. Reflect on your values, your passions, your aspirations. What do you believe in? What do you stand for? What is your life's purpose?

Once you've defined your truth, find ways to express it. It could be through your words, your actions, your creativity, your relationships. Speak your mind, even when your voice shakes. Act in alignment with your values, even when it's challenging. Create art that reflects your soul, even when it's raw and vulnerable. Build relationships that honor your true self, even if it means setting boundaries.

Remember, expressing your truth is not about pleasing others or fitting in. It's about honoring your authentic self, standing in your power, embodying the Divine Feminine. It's about singing your unique song, dancing your unique dance, and living your unique life.

Making Decisions Aligned with Your Values

Think of life as a grand puzzle, with each decision acting as a piece that fits into the larger picture of who we are. Whether it's choosing a career path, forming relationships, or pursuing personal passions, each decision contributes to the intricate design of our lives. Making decisions in harmony with our values is like selecting puzzle pieces that seamlessly integrate into the overall picture, forming a mosaic that represents the essence of our true selves. Just as each piece of a puzzle is essential to completing the image, every decision we make shapes the unique and beautiful mosaic of our life's journey.

Our values are our guiding principles, our moral compass, our inner standards. They define what matters to us, what brings us fulfillment, and what aligns with our true selves. Making decisions aligned with our values ensures that our actions reflect our authentic self, and resonate with our Divine Feminine essence.

To make value-aligned decisions, start by defining your core values. What principles guide your life? What values resonate with your true self? What values reflect your Divine Feminine essence?

Once you've defined your values, use them as a compass for your decisions. Before making a decision, check in with your values. Does this choice align with your values? Does it reflect your authentic self? Does it serve your highest good?

Remember, making value-aligned decisions may not always be easy. Sometimes, it involves choosing the harder path, the road less traveled. But as you align your decisions with your values, you align your life with your true self, your Divine Feminine essence. You create a life that resonates with your authentic melody, your unique rhythm, your beautiful dance.

Living authentically is like lighting a candle in the darkness, illuminating your path with the radiant glow of your true self. It involves recognizing and honoring your feelings, expressing your truth, and making decisions aligned with your values. As you embrace this authentic living, you embody the Divine Feminine, transforming your life into a beautiful symphony of authenticity, alignment, and fulfillment. As you continue to explore the Divine Feminine in the chapters ahead, may this symphony guide you, inspire you, and empower you. May it remind you of the beauty, the power, the grace of the Divine Feminine, resonating within you and all around you.

Chapter Twelve

Divine Feminine: Becoming the Pathmaker

As we turn the page to this last chapter, we find ourselves standing at such a threshold, poised to venture into the realm of self-discovery. With each step, we will explore, understand, and cherish our unique gifts and strengths, honor our personal journey, and embrace our evolving identity.

Embracing Your Unique Path

Acknowledging Your Unique Gifts and Strengths

Each of us possesses unique gifts and strengths that make us who we are, and contribute to the beauty of the world around us.

Your gifts could be your ability to listen empathetically to a friend, your creative flair in cooking, your knack for making people laugh, or your resilience in the face of adversity. No gift is too small or too insignificant. Each one is a precious gem that adds sparkle to your being.

Take a moment now to acknowledge your gifts. You might want to make a list, jotting down all the qualities and skills that make you unique. As you do this, let yourself feel a sense of pride and appreciation for these gifts. They are your superpowers, your guiding stars, your Divine Feminine essence.

Honoring Your Personal Journey

Each of us walks a unique path in life, a path marked by our experiences, choices, and lessons. This path, with its peaks and valleys, its twists and turns, defines our personal journey.

Consider a mountain range. Each mountain, with its unique shape, height, and terrain, symbolizes our individual journeys. Some mountains are rugged with steep cliffs, others are gentle with lush green slopes. Each mountain bears the scars of weather and time, just as we bear the marks of our experiences.

Just as a mountain climber pauses to appreciate the view from the summit, take a moment to honor your personal journey. Reflect on your experiences, your struggles, and your victories. Cherish your growth, your resilience, your progress. Recognize the wisdom you've gained, the strength you've cultivated, the person you've become.

Embracing Your Evolving Identity

In the grand tapestry of life, each thread represents an aspect of our identity. Our experiences, relationships, beliefs, dreams, and values weave together to form our unique pattern. As we journey through life, new threads are added, old ones fade, and our pattern evolves.

Consider the flame of a candle, flickering and dancing in the darkness. The flame is like our evolving identity, constantly shifting and transforming. Just as the flame is shaped by the currents of air around it, our identity is influenced by the circumstances and people in our lives. Embrace this fluidity, this perpetual dance of change.

Celebrate the person you are becoming, guided by your experiences, shaped by your choices, and inspired by your dreams. As you do so, you embody the dynamic, resilient, and transformative energy of the Divine Feminine. You become the flame, casting light and warmth on your journey, illuminating the path ahead with grace, authenticity, and purpose.

As you step onto the path of self-discovery, let the Divine Feminine be your compass, guiding you towards your authentic self, your unique potential, and your inner Goddess. With each step, may you discover a new aspect of yourself, a new strength, a new joy. And as you journey, may you find the courage to embrace your unique path, honor your personal journey, and celebrate your evolving identity. For in this journey, you are not just walking a path, you are becoming the pathmaker, carving your own path with the strength, wisdom, and grace of the Divine Feminine.

Overcoming Obstacles with Grace

Cultivating Resilience

Imagine a flexible willow tree, its slender branches swaying gracefully in the wind. Despite the strongest gusts, the willow bends but never breaks, embodying the power of resilience. As we navigate our path, we too will encounter winds of adversity and challenges that test our strength and resolve. The key to facing these challenges lies in cultivating resilience, the capacity to recover quickly, to adapt, to bounce back with grace.

Resilience is not inborn, but a skill that can be nurtured and grown. One way to cultivate resilience is through mindfulness. By staying present, we can respond to challenges rather than react, making choices that serve our highest good. Another way is by nurturing a positive outlook. By focusing on solutions rather than problems, we empower ourselves to overcome obstacles.

Self-care is another crucial aspect of resilience. By taking care of our physical, emotional, and mental well-being, we replenish our resources and enhance our capacity to cope with stress.

Learning from Challenges

Each challenge we encounter, and each obstacle we overcome, shapes us, revealing more of our authentic selves, our inner strength, and our divine essence.

Challenges, although difficult, hold valuable lessons. They teach us about our strengths and weaknesses, our values and beliefs, our dreams and desires. They push us out of our comfort zone, forcing us to grow, to evolve, to transform.

To learn from challenges, we need to embrace them as opportunities for growth. Instead of resisting the challenge, we can ask ourselves, "What is this challenge teaching me? What can I learn from this experience?" By adopting this mindset, we transform challenges into stepping stones, leading us closer to our true self, our Divine Feminine essence.

Seeking Support When Needed

No matter how strong or independent we may be, there are times when we need support. It could be emotional support, a listening ear, a comforting word. Or practical support, advice, resources, or assistance. Navigating the journey of single parenthood, I've often found it difficult to ask for assistance. Fear of burdening my loved ones and the desire to prove my independence have weighed heavily on my shoulders. Yet, embracing the nurturing energy of the Divine Feminine has been transformative. It's taught me to release the notion of self-sufficiency and embrace the beauty of receiving support without guilt or shame.

Seeking support is not a sign of weakness, but a testament to our strength. It takes courage to admit we need help, to reach out to others, to share our struggles. When we seek support, we open ourselves to the wisdom, strength, and compassion of others. We create a circle of support, a sisterhood of strength, embodying the collective power of the Divine Feminine.

In the dance of life, challenges are the steps that test our grace, our strength, and our resilience. They are the rhythm that shapes our dance, the melody that sings our song. As we embrace these challenges, may we dance with grace, sing with joy, and live with authenticity. May we embody the Divine Feminine, transforming obstacles into opportunities, challenges into triumphs, and dreams into reality.

Celebrating Your Progress

Recognizing Small Wins

Consider an artist meticulously crafting a mosaic. Each tiny piece of tile, each speck of color, each subtle shade, plays an essential role in creating the final masterpiece. Similarly, every small win in your life - a kind word spoken, a negative thought replaced, a fear faced - is a vital part of your masterpiece, your Divine Feminine journey.

To recognize these small wins, cultivate an awareness of your daily actions, thoughts, and emotions. At the end of each day, take a few moments to reflect on these small victories. Perhaps you made a healthy food choice, or you took a step towards a personal goal, or you handled a difficult situation with grace. No win is too small to celebrate.

Reflecting on Your Growth

Growth is like a seed sprouting into a tree. It starts small, barely noticeable, but with time and nurturing, it unfolds into a magnificent manifestation of life. As you walk the path of the Divine Feminine, your growth may seem slow or subtle, but rest assured, every step you take, every choice you make, contributes to your evolution.

Reflection is a powerful tool to acknowledge this growth. It provides a mirror to see how far you've come, to appreciate the changes within you, to celebrate your evolution.

Start a reflection ritual. It could be weekly, monthly, or yearly. Create a quiet, sacred space for this ritual. Light a candle, play some soothing music, make yourself a cup of tea. Then, close your eyes and take a journey down memory lane. Recall where you were at the start of this period and compare it to where you are now. What changes do you notice? How have you grown? What have you learned?

Rewarding Yourself

In the hustle and bustle of life, we often forget to pause and treat ourselves. Rewarding yourself is an integral part of the Divine Feminine journey. It's a way to honor your efforts, to fuel your motivation, to celebrate your Divine Feminine essence.

Rewards come in all shapes and sizes. It could be a relaxing bath at the end of a long day, a favorite book read under a cozy blanket, or a nature walk on a sunny afternoon. It could be a special treat, a new outfit, or a day trip to a place you love.

The key is to choose rewards that bring you joy, that resonate with your soul, that make you feel loved and cherished. As you reward yourself, you strengthen your connection with the Divine Feminine, nurturing your sense of self-love, self-worth, and self-appreciation.

In the grand dance of life, every step, every twirl, every leap, tells a story of progress, of growth, of transformation. As you dance to the rhythm of the Divine Feminine, may you celebrate your progress, your small wins, your growth. May you reward yourself, cherishing your efforts, your journey, your Divine Feminine essence. And as you do so, may you dance with joy, with grace, with love, under the radiant glow of the Divine Feminine.

The Journey Continues: Embracing the Unknown

Cultivating Trust in the Process

The path ahead is uncharted, filled with mystery and uncertainty. Yet, it's within this uncertainty that the magic of transformation resides.

Life is an adventure, much like embarking on a journey through uncharted terrain. The Divine Feminine beckons you to embrace this spirit of adventure, to boldly step into the unknown. It's about surrendering to the unpredictable twists and turns of the journey, relinquishing the urge to control or foresee the outcome. Just as an intrepid explorer surrenders to the thrill of discovery, allow yourself to surrender to the exhilarating flow of life's adventure.

Trusting the process might seem daunting, but it's much like floating. You need to relax and trust the water to support you. Similarly, to trust in life's process, you need to relax and trust that the universe is supporting you. This trust becomes a beacon, guiding you through the shadows of the unknown, illuminating your path with the gentle light of the Divine Feminine.

Staying Open to New Experiences

Imagine yourself as a delicate flower bud, once closed and guarded, yet holding the potential for exquisite beauty within.

Despite my past heartaches, failed relationships, and the scars they've left, I've persevered. I recently walked away from a relationship because I was giving more than was being reciprocated. I was settling for less than what I desired. Although ending it was uncomfortable and frightening, the loss ultimately proved to be a gain. A friend said to me "Just because your heart hurts right now, don't close it off."

Dear loves, please keep your heart open to the possibility of love and connection.

Just as the sun gently encourages the bud to unfurl its petals, allow yourself to remain vulnerable, to soften, and to let love in. It's through this resilience and willingness to embrace the unknown that you begin to blossom, revealing the strength and beauty that lies within.

Despite the risks and uncertainties, you continue to say 'yes' to love, bravely stepping into new relationships and experiences, even amidst the pain and hurt of the past. It's in this openness to growth and transformation that you find the courage to unfurl into your full potential, knowing that each new bloom is a testament to your strength and resilience.

This openness is not about recklessness or blindly accepting every opportunity. It's about discerning which experiences resonate with our soul, with our Divine Feminine essence. It's about being curious, being adventurous, being willing to learn and grow. As we stay open to new experiences, we allow life to surprise us, to teach us, to transform us, and in doing so, we dance with the rhythm of the Divine Feminine.

Embracing Change with Courage

Just as the caterpillar undergoes a remarkable metamorphosis, emerging from its cocoon as a beautiful butterfly, humans too experience transformations throughout their lives. Metamorphosis is a stark reminder of the power of change. It's a testament to the potential that lies within each of us, the potential to transform, to evolve, to soar to new heights.

Embracing change with courage is about acknowledging the inevitability of change and choosing to dance with it, rather than resist it. It's about viewing change not as a threat, but as an invitation to grow, to evolve, to transform.

Of course, change can be challenging. It can bring uncertainty, discomfort, and even fear. But it also brings growth, renewal, and transformation. It's the wind that propels our sails, the current that carries us to new shores, and the rhythm that shapes our Divine Feminine dance.

As we navigate the winding path of the Divine Feminine, we are not merely passive travelers. We become pioneers, pathfinders, trailblazers. We learn to trust the process, to stay open to new experiences, and to embrace change with courage. We learn to dance with the rhythm of life, to sing our unique song, to paint our unique masterpiece. And as we dance, sing, and paint, we embody the Divine Feminine, transforming our lives into a beautiful symphony of authenticity, courage, and grace.

As we continue this exploration, I invite you to join me in this dance, to add your unique notes to this symphony, to contribute your unique strokes to this masterpiece. May the Divine Feminine guide us, inspire us, and empower us on this journey. And may we, in turn, inspire, empower, and uplift others, creating a ripple effect of transformation, celebration, and love.

Conclusion

EMBRACING THE DIVINE FEMININE WITHIN

As we find ourselves at the end of this sacred exploration into the Divine Feminine, I want to take a moment to honor the journey we've embarked on together. Like a river that has wound its way through vast landscapes, we've navigated through valleys and peaks, explored tranquil pools and braved roaring rapids. Each chapter, each word, each thought was a stepping stone on this transformative path.

You've opened your heart to the lessons from the Divine Feminine, embracing her qualities of intuition, compassion, creativity, and resilience. You've discovered the power of vulnerability, the strength in softness, the wisdom in stillness. You've learned to honor the cycles of nature, to dance with the rhythm of life, to flow with grace and ease. You've cultivated self-love, self-care, and self-acceptance, nurturing your body, mind, and spirit.

This book was an invitation, a call to the sacred journey of embracing the Divine Feminine within you. A journey that isn't a destination to be reached but a path to be walked, a dance to be danced, a song to be sung. It's a journey that invites you to dive deep into the ocean of your being, to uncover the hidden treasures of your soul, to awaken the Goddess within you.

I've been privileged enough to be a guide on this journey, but the path you've walked, the growth you've experienced, the transformation you've undergone - it's all your own. Your courage, your openness, your willingness to explore the unknown - they've been your compass, your beacon, your guiding star.

As you continue to walk this path, remember to honor the Goddess within you. She is your true essence, your authentic self, your Divine Feminine. She is the river that flows within you, the mountain that stands within you, the sky that expands within you. She is you - beautiful, powerful, divine.

My wish for you, dear reader, is that you continue to embrace the Divine Feminine, to dance her dance, to sing her song, to shine her light. May you honor her in your daily rituals, embody her in your interactions, express her in your creativity. May you wear her strength as your armor, her wisdom as your guide, her love as your beacon.

And as you do, may you inspire others - women and men alike - to embark on their own journey towards the Divine Feminine. May your light ignite their light, your dance inspire their dance, your song echo in their song. For the Divine Feminine isn't just about empowering women, it's about transforming the world - one heart, one soul, one step at a time.

Remember, this conclusion isn't an end, but rather a new beginning. It's a stepping stone to the next chapter of your journey, a doorway to the next landscape of your exploration, a threshold to the next level of your growth. As you step across this threshold, know that you carry with you the blessings of the Divine Feminine, the wisdom of your experiences, and the power of your potential.

So, as we part ways on this page, I want you to remember one thing: you are not just walking a path, you are the path. You are not just learning from the Divine Feminine, you are the Divine Feminine. You are not just becoming the Goddess, you are the Goddess. You are, and always have been, a manifestation of the Divine Feminine. And as you embrace this truth, may you dance with joy, shine with love, and soar with grace into the infinite sky of your Divine Feminine journey.

With all my love and blessings,

Heather

xo

Your Reviews Matter

A Lifeline for Authors

Dear Reader,

Your reviews on platforms like Amazon and Goodreads mean the world to authors like me. They are not just a gesture of encouragement; they are my love language, connecting me deeply with my readers.

Each review you leave serves as a guidepost for others, helping them discover stories and shaping the literary landscape. For self-published authors, your feedback is especially vital—it's a lifeline that sustains our craft and allows us to reach wider audiences.

If my story has touched you in any way, I kindly ask you to consider leaving a review on Amazon. Your words, however brief, carry immense weight and meaning, shaping both my future works and the experiences of other readers.

Thank you for being a part of this journey and for considering my humble request.

With heartfelt gratitude,
Heather
xo

A Gift for my Readers

As you journey through the pages of this book, I want to offer you more than just words on a page—I want to provide you with tools to enhance your well-being and enrich your life.

That's why I'm excited to share with you a resource that goes hand in hand with the themes explored in this book:

3-Day Mini-Video Series to Pelvic Freedom: *Rediscover Your Confidence and Radiance*

To access this invaluable resource, visit the following link: https://www.heatheronhealth.com/pages/pelvicfreedom

The Embodiment of Boundaries

To access this transformative practice, simply visit the following link: https://www.heatheronhealth.com/pages/embodiment-of-boundaries

References

Academy, E. A. (2023, July 26). *The feminine Archetypal wheel.* Embodied Awakening Academy. https://embodiedawakeningacademy.com/the-feminine-archetypal-wheel/

Amabile, T. M. (2020, May 6). *The power of small wins.* Harvard Business Review. https://hbr.org/2011/05/the-power-of-small-wins

Ayesha. (2021, June 23). *An explanation of the 7 Feminine Archetypes - Women Love Power®.* Women Love Power®. https://womenlovepower.com/an-explanation-of-the-7-basic-feminine-archetypes/

Berkheiser, K. (2024, March 27). *10 Foods high in phytoestrogens.* Healthline. https://www.healthline.com/nutrition/foods-with-estrogen

CARE. (2024, February 27). *Women & Girls' Safe Spaces: A Promising Practices Guide - CARE.* http://www.care.org/news-and-stories/resources/women-girls-safe-spaces-a-promising-practices-guide/

Clinic, C. (2024, April 10). *Self-Care isn't selfish: 17 tips for making yourself a Priority.* Cleveland Clinic. https://health.clevelandclinic.org/why-self-care-isnt-selfish-advice-for-women/

Connors, H. (2023, December 29). Living a life of meaning: the benefits of intentional living. *The Intention Habit.* https://theintentionhabit.com/benefits-of-intentional-living/

Developing your Self-Care Plan. (2019, October 28). University at Buffalo School of Social Work - University at Buffalo. https://socialwork.buffalo.edu/resources/self-care-starter-kit/developing-your-self-care-plan.html

Divine Union: when God joins a man and a woman together. (2023, December 3). Tabernacles Central. https://www.thefinalfeast.com/divine-marriage/

Dunfee, S. (2023, February 21). *Empowering energy of the divine feminine*. Chopra. https://chopra.com/articles/empowering-energy-of-the-divine-feminine

Embracing your feminine energy is the secret to a strong relationship. (2023, November 6). Evie Magazine. https://www.eviemagazine.com/post/embracing-your-feminine-energy-is-the-secret-to-a-strong-relationship

Fitness, M. M. (2022, August 2). *Personal strengths and powerful outcomes*. Get Mentally Fit. https://www.getmentallyfit.com.au/using-personal-strengths-for-powerful-outcomes/

Goddard, N. (2021a). *The power of awareness: The Power of Awareness: Neville Goddard's Popular Self-help book - Unlocking Inner Potential: Neville Goddard's Guide to Harnessing the Power of Awareness*. Prabhat Prakashan.

Goddard, N. (2021b). *Your faith is your fortune*. Prabhat Prakashan.

Gosia. (2022, August 29). 5 Ways to awaken the divine feminine within you and live in harmony and balance. *Medium*. https://medium.com/mystic-minds/5-ways-to-awaken-the-divine-feminine-within-you-and-live-in-harmony-and-balance-befa17bdc74f

Gray, J. (2023, December 10). *8 Powerful exercises to increase your feminine energy*. Jordan Gray Consulting. https://www.jordangrayconsulting.com/8-powerful-exercises-increase-feminine-energy/

Gurukul, L. (2023, June 17). *Embracing the Divine Feminine: Beyond gender Stereotypes — LEELA*. LEELA. https://www.leelagurukul.com/blog/embracing-the-divine-feminine-beyond-gender-stereotypes

Howard, L. (2021, February 25). *16 yoga poses to ignite your feminine energy - YOGA PRACTICE*. YOGA PRACTICE. https://yogapractice.com/yoga/feminine-energy/

Karageorgi, S. (2023, March 17). *The Divine Feminine: 8 ancient forms of the Great Mother Goddess*. TheCollector. https://www.thecollector.com/divine-feminine-ancient-art/

Kathryn Garcia: The Feminine Divine - Exhibitions - GAVLAK. (n.d.). https://www.gavlakgallery.com/exhibitions/kathryn-garcia-the-feminine-divine

Kaur, R. (2023, December 14). Women need a sisterhood: finding more success by supporting each other. *Forbes*. https://www.forbes.com/sites/forbescoachescouncil/2020/11/10/women-need-a-sisterhood-finding-more-success-by-supporting-each-other/

Lancer, D. (2021, December 11). The Power of Authenticity: 6 Steps to Achieve it. - Becoming You - Medium. *Medium*. https://medium.com/becoming-you/the-power-of-authenticity-6-steps-to-achieve-it-a177aa513e41

Leicht, C., Gocłowska, M. A., Van Breen, J., De Lemus, S., & De Moura, G. R. (2017). Counter-Stereotypes and feminism promote leadership aspirations in highly identified women. *Frontiers in Psychology, 8*. https://doi.org/10.3389/fpsyg.2017.00883

Lmhc, S. B. (2023, December 12). *Sensual vs. Sexual: Understanding the Differences*. Choosing Therapy. https://www.choosingtherapy.com/sensual-vs-sexual/

McFarland. (2023, February 19). *The Divine Feminine in Ancient Europe - McFarland*. https://mcfarlandbooks.com/product/the-divine-feminine-in-ancient-europe/

MindTools | Home. (n.d.). https://www.mindtools.com/ak3zuv5/intuition-and-decision-making

Pmp, K. C. M. B. (2023, May 19). *Sympathy vs. Empathy: What's the Difference?* Verywell Mind. https://www.verywellmind.com/sympathy-vs-empathy-whats-the-difference-7496474

Psychologist, J. S. B. (2024, March 8). *Exploring the body mind Connection (Incl. 5 techniques)*. PositivePsychology.com. https://positivepsychology.com/body-mind-integration-attention-training/

Resilience: Build skills to endure hardship. (2023, December 23). Mayo Clinic. https://www.mayoclinic.org/tests-procedures/resilience-training/in-depth/resilience/art-20046311

Ruether, R. R. (2005a). *Goddesses and the Divine Feminine*. https://doi.org/10.1525/california/9780520231467.001.0001

Ruether, R. R. (2005b). *Goddesses and the Divine Feminine*. https://doi.org/10.1525/california/9780520231467.001.0001

Sampson, G., & Sampson, G. (2022, January 20). 19 Powerful Spiritual Self-Care Practices for Better Spiritual Health - in its season. *In Its Season - Living Simply and Authentically in Every Season of Life*. https://initsseason.com/spiritual-health-and-wellness/

Shah, P. (2020, June 16). *How to balance and harmonize masculine and feminine energies*. Chopra. https://www.chopra.com/articles/how-to-balance-and-harmonize-masculine-and-feminine-energies

Smith, M., MA. (2024, February 5). *Setting healthy boundaries in relationships*. HelpGuide.org. https://www.helpguide.org/articles/relationships-communication/setting-healthy-boundaries-in-relationships.htm

Standard, H. N. (2024, January 9). *How to practice resilience as a woman leader*. Her New Standard. https://hernewstandard.com/how-to-practice-resilience-as-a-leader/

Stinson, N. (2019, September 23). *10 steps to develop an Abundance Mindset*. Chopra. https://chopra.com/articles/10-steps-to-develop-an-abundance-mindset

Van Horn Mcmhc Lpc-C, H., & Van Horn Mcmhc Lpc-C, H. (2023, August 17). *Journaling to Heal: Effective writing Strategies and Methods*. Day One | Your Journal for Life. https://dayoneapp.com/blog/journaling-to-heal/

Weir, K. (n.d.). *Forgiveness can improve mental and physical health*. https://www.apa.org. https://www.apa.org/monitor/2017/01/ce-corner

Women, Ritual, and Power on JSTOR. (n.d.). *www.jstor.org*. https://www.jstor.org/stable/3346820

About the Author

Heather's journey as a healer and advocate for holistic wellness is deeply intertwined with her role as a single mother, a facet of her life that has profoundly shaped her understanding of the divine feminine. For 14 years, she served as a nurse, driven by her passion for holistic health and her innate ability to connect with others on a profound level. Within the walls of her nursing practice, she found solace in listening to the stories of those she cared for, offering not just medical support, but a compassionate presence that embraced the entirety of each person.

Even before her nursing career, Heather found herself drawn to the practice of yoga, a discipline she has both embraced and shared as an instructor since 2006. Her journey into yoga, particularly Kundalini yoga, served as a powerful complement to her medical background, culminating in her unique expertise in pelvic floor yoga.

DIVINE FEMININE UNVEILED

Yet, beyond her professional endeavors, Heather's life as a single mother has been a catalyst for her own healing journey. It's through this journey that she has come to embrace the divine feminine within herself, finding strength and resilience in her role as both nurturer and provider. Her commitment to living "outside of the box" is not just a personal ethos but a mission to challenge societal norms and dismantle the taboos and shame that shroud so many aspects of our lives.

In her moments of respite, Heather finds joy in dance, song, and the simple pleasures of spending time with her children and beloved pets. She is unafraid to explore her own healing through plant medicine and sensual expression, recognizing the power of nature and art to facilitate inner transformation.

Ultimately, Heather's message is one of empowerment and liberation. Through her work, she seeks to grant both men and women the permission to shed their shame, transcend their anxieties, and rediscover their inherent radiance. Her life is a testament to the transformative power of embracing one's true self and finding healing in the embrace of the divine feminine.

Also by Heather Dolson

Find Heather's books on Amazon and audiobooks on Audible.

www.ingramcontent.com/pod-product-compliance
Lightning Source LLC
Chambersburg PA
CBHW052142070526
44585CB00017B/1945